CELTIC HERITAGE PRE
WOODSIDE, NEW

G000146458

&

THE AODH RUADH Ó DOMHNAILL GUILD
TAPPEN, NORTH DAKOTA

LIBRARY of CONGRESS CATALOGUE CARD NUMBER: 86-72169

ISBN: 0-9614753-2-3

Cover: cross from the monastic site on Skellig Michael,
Co Kerry.

PREFACE

Interest in the early phases of Christianity in Ireland is often discouraged by inaccessibility of sources for scholar as well as layman and the difficulties encountered in interpreting them. There is also the fact that the early medieval period is largely ignored by high school and college curricula; or worse, often treated with contempt. Self-serving 20th-century intellectuals have for decades "reinterpreted" historical data and side-stepped contemporary failings by assigning modern barbarism the rubric "medieval." The effort before the reader was undertaken in part to somewhat remedy such problems and distortions.

While not stinting in scholarship, the author has attempted to encourage readers by incorporating specialist references in the text. All such are fully listed, with pertinent abbreviations, in the bibliography.

The author would like to thank the City University of New York's PSC-CUNY Research Award Program for two grants which greatly facilitated his efforts. Appreciation is also due Jennifer Lonigan who patiently drew the maps for this study. The author must also mark his indebtedness to Mary Kovar, Librarian of the Montgomery Free Library, Montgomery, New York, for her thoroughness, patience and sense of humor, and without whose aid many a scholarly material would not have been so easily found.

Spring 1985

P.R.L.

I would like to express my appreciation to Celtic Heritage Press for having decided to produce this second, much corrected edition of the EARLY IRISH CHURCH.

Fall 1986

P.R.L.

I wish to offer my thanks to Shirley Starke for all of her kind assistance in this third printing, and to the Aodh Ruadh Ó Domhnaill Guild for the sponsorship of the project.

FALL 1988

P.R.L

TABLE OF CONTENTS

FROM THE DESERT TO IRELAND

Before speaking of the monastic church in Ireland we must consider its sources. To do so we start with the Near East. An Egyptian Copt, known to the world as Anthony the Hermit (c. 251-356), chose to separate himself from the world of corruption and to devote his labors to the contemplation of God. His life and sayings were not only to inspire many Christians of his age but also to set down roots for flowering the movement of solitary devotion called "monasticism" (Gk. monos-- "one"). During his stay in the desert Anthony was to gain followers and visitors to his place of ascetic experience (askesis--"training"). One who came under Anthony's influence--although we are not clear as to his relation to the master--was Pachomius who wrote the first Rule for the organization of a monastic community, that is for cenobites (koinos-- "common";bios--"life").The "rule" was to enjoy much popularity in the western world for the fact that it was translated into Latin by no less a figure than Saint Jerome (c. 340-420).

The great Athanasius of Alexandria (c. 296-373), pillar of orthodoxy, was also taken with the humble hermit, to the degree that he saw fit to compose the definitive (if highly idealized and literarily conventional) Life of Anthony (Lietzmann, IV, 135), a study of extreme asceticism, touching personal pronouncements, visions, foreknowledge, command of wild beasts, and pursuit of the Pythagorean mandate to regain primal innocence. It was in Latin translation--probably that of Evagrius of Antioch--that the Life circulated through Europe as a result of one of Athanasius' many exiles to Gaul during the religious quarrels of the mid-fourth century.

It must be understood that the movement to ascetic perfection was not, as such, an exclusively Christian phenomenon. Many cultures through recorded history have displayed variations on the theme: Pythagoreans, the immured in the temple of Memphis in the second century B.C., Essenes, Buddhists What, in the minds of scholars such as Lietzmann (p. 132), did become unique in the Christian context was a separation of the devout from the rest of the world. As scriptural support for such an existence one need but consult the story of John the Baptist as well as Jesus' command to the rich young man: "Sell all that you own and distribute the money to the poor, and you will have treasure in heaven; then come and follow me" (Luke 18, 22-23). To this one might object that John did not, for all his self-denial, totally shun the company of men. In fact, his denunciation of evil led to his death

And following Jesus would not have brought one to avoid the presence of others. The fact is, as implied, there were two (not mutually exclusive) modes of monasticism: the anchoritic (anakhorein--"to retire") and the cenobitic, or communal. The former, while often located in cells of meditation near a foundation of the latter, did remain apart from mankind; the latter did, as we shall see, associate with those outside their group, often to the degree of conflict and annoyance.

In addition to its pious motives, the movement may be looked upon as containing reform elements. Over a generation before Anthony's death the Church had been granted official toleration with the proclamation of the Emperor Constantine's so-called Edict of Milan in 313. Thereafter a major portion of the Church's energies had been spent in doctrinal squabbles, heated infighting and the search for orthodoxy. To some, therefore, monasticism must have appeared as a return to the original message of Christ and the apostles. To others, bent upon maintaining ecclesiastical order in a Church called upon to play an increasingly important role in shoring up the breaches of empire, it must have seemed at least a potentially dangerous manifestation of erratic individuality; in particular when it became apparent that some monks felt no compunction about roaming free to do their work as they saw it and/or to denounce corruption as they perceived it. It was an age of great minds, great activity and looming peril.

Monasticism's reception was, therefore, to some degree ambivalent. It received the enthusiastic support of the great names of the 4th and early 5th centuries: Jerome, Ambrose of Milan (333-397), Augustine of Hippo (354-430),as well as popes Damasus (r. 366-384) and Siricius (384-398). Still, from the time of the Egyptian desert and throughout its history, the movement had displayed conflict between officialdom (meaning most often bishops) and its wandering-prone members. On one occasion the source of trouble was the brothers' primitive, anthropomorphic simplicity of belief which brought opposition from Bishop Theophilus of Alexandria in 399. The result was violence and some rioting. Later, after 400, even the great John Chrysostom (c. 345-407) was not immune to expulsion from his see in Constantinople, due in part to his growing unpopularity for having favored foreign monks in ecclesiastical appointments. Throughout the late Low Empire (5th century) and through the early medieval period (varying from region to region, but surely till the time of Charlemagne who reigned from 800-814 as Holy Roman Emperor) the Church would repeatedly insist on the maintenance of discipline and order in the face of impending chaos--including efforts to curtail monastic independence. One of the clearest and firmest sets of guidelines was drawn up at the universal Church meeting or Council of Chalcedon (451) which commanded monastic submission in all ways to episcopal authority and forbade monks to leave their monasteries and to enter in any way into either ecclesiastical or secular affairs. In an empire undergoing the strains of decay and in a church attempting to hold soul and world together, the monks, for all their sympathy-inspiring selflessness, must have truly tested the patience of authority.

If such were not food enough for conflict, monasticism from its early days was associated somewhat with names suspected of unorthodox views. This troubled the ranks of the movement's supporters and also deepened suspicion among its detractors. John Cassian (c. 360-435), who wrote during the period 420-430 (Cassian, p. 8), passing on to the West many of the sayings of the desert Fathers, composed in the 18th of his Conferences what has been called "the first known history of monasticism" (Cassian, 51). His influence would extend eventually to continental, British and Irish monastics alike; and, though exonerated by history, he was nonetheless exposed to the influences of Origenism (named for the great Alexandrian scholar Origenes Adamantius, d.254, whose vast and enormously complex works apparently included the doctrine of the preexistence of souls) which had impressed not only one of Cassian's masters, Paphnutius, under whose direction the former had spent some time in the desert, but Cassian's patron John Chrysostom as well. Origenism was condemned by the Council of Alexandria (400), but not before having been supported by Pope Siricius (d.398), condemned by his successor Anastasius (d.401) and being the cause of transforming the friendship of Jerome and Rufinus into intractable hatred.

Cassian was involved in still another theological controversy: Pelagianism. This heresy, occidental in scope and British in origin, is more directly pertinent to the question of religion and monasticism in the Western Isles. Deriving its title from Pelagius Bretto (d. circa 408-9) little of whose works remains, this concept contended that man was capable of achieving salvation through free will and denied what has been viewed by some as the fatalism of Augustine of Hippo. The fur-

or resulting from Pelagius' thought included an ongoing debate
between Augustine's forces (including Prosper of Aquitaine,
later to be papal chronicler, d. circa 461) and those of Cassian and the monastic community of Marseilles. Again, this
was an issue both complex and emotion-charged; suffice it to
say that as the dust of centuries subsided so also faded many
of the allegations and counter-allegations of the adversar-
ies. Capital to our subject is that the issue was considered grave enough to have repercussions extending to the Western Isles--both Britain and Ireland--and caused church leaders to find it necessary to send emissaries who might combat
it wherever encountered.

Meanwhile in Gaul, the unquestionably orthodox Hilary of
Poitiers (c. 315-368), who had contacts with the East due to
his exile to Phrygia for having supported Athanasius in still
another theological dispute, sponsored and trained a former
Pannonian (Hungarian) soldier whom the world was to know as
Martin of Tours (c. 316-397). Martin's piety, deeds and devotion to the poor found their most famous popularization in
Sulpicius Severus' Life of Martin, apparently composed even
before the good man's death. It has been suggested that this
Life was intended to rival and replace in popularity Athanasius' Life of Anthony (P&L, p. 272). It seems certain that
Martin approached legendary stature in his own time. His community at Ligugé (near Poitiers) held some traits disturbing
for Church authorities, among them Martin's insistence upon
carrying his mission to the peasants. As a monastic and re-
luctant bishop Martin geared his efforts to ministering to
the poor and all but ignored his diocesan-minded colleagues.
His attitude reminds one of Cassian recommending avoidance
of bishops who by their offices must be concerned with this-
worldly things; it also recalls the desert ascetics who sometimes violently resisted episcopal consecration (Cassian, 27
& 68). This spirit of independence shown by those under monastic rule (and hence called "regular clergy": Latin, re-
gula--"rule") and the countering discomfort experienced by
their secular counterparts (saeculum--"world") was to find
its way into the Irish Church and would surface at various
times and in various circumstances.

A disciple of Martin, Victricius of Rouen (another former
soldier) continued his master's mission and apparently visited Britain toward the end of the 4th century. According to
Victricius himself (Morris, 352f.), he was appealed to by his

fellow bishops to aid in the settlement of a dispute, the nature of which we do not know. What is clear is that his actions prompted Pope Innocent I (r. 401-17) to admonish Victricius concerning church discipline and Rome's rights in resolving controversy. It was Innocent's reign which saw the undeniable beginning of the end for the Empire: the breaching of Roman defences on the Rhine by the Vandals, the Suevi and the Alans (406); the temporary repulsion of the Visigoths by the Romanized Vandal Stilicho in the same year; the Visigothic siege of Rome in 408 after Stilicho's murder by Emperor Honorius; and the sack of Rome by Alaric's Visigoths in 410. Britain itself was experiencing turmoil. In approximately 407 Constantius II, proclaimed emperor by rebellious British troops, crossed into Gaul to make good his claim, only to meet defeat by Honorius' army near Arles in 411. Constantius' actions appear to be the last major stripping of Britain's Roman forces, for in 410 Honorius informed the British chieftains that their fate was in their own hands. With empire wasted, heterodoxy afoot and differences within her ranks, the Church of Innocent must never have had so great a need of discipline.

In Britain Christianity had a substantial, if at first unclear, tradition. As early as 314 (only one year after the Edict of Milan) British bishops are in attendance at the Council of Arles, called to establish discipline and standardize the ever-poignant dating of Easter. Perhaps Christianity had arrived in Britain at some date early in the 2nd century—either with legionnaires or tradesmen, or both. We do have the cursory boast of Tertullian (circa 200) claiming the presence of Christians in places inaccessible to Romans; and Origen's remark (c. 240) referring to Britons being unified by Christianity (D&C, 167ff.). In his Ecclesiastical History, Bede, following the tradition of Constantius' Life of Germanus (5th century), Gildas' Destruction and Conquest of Britain (mid-6th century), as well as Venantius Fortunatus' In Praise of Virgins (late 6th century), devotes the 7th chapter of Book I to the martyrdom of Saint Alban which Bede (writing in the 8th century) places during the persecution of Diocletian (r. 284-305).

As to the physical remains of early British Christianity, much of it is found in the outlying regions of the West, in the South, and in what today is northern England (D&C, 170-3). Just how much of Christianity was destroyed and/or displaced by post-Roman Germanic invasion is a matter of speculation. What appears certain is that the Faith, once established,had a tradition continuous from Roman times: the fact that Britain's bishops regularly attended gatherings of the universal Church from the time of Constantine would appear as insurmountable proof of this. By the end of the Roman era in Britain, the Church there was Roman in character and enjoyed a reputation for orthodoxy.

A decade before the end of Roman rule and in an area apparently west of the limits of Hadrian's wall, there labored among the southern Picts a man of British (i.e. Celtic) birth called Ninian. His community was located at Whithorn near the Mull of Galloway. What we know of him we receive from Bede (EH, II 4) who tells us of the holyman's origin, that he was a bishop educated in Rome, and that his see was extraordinary for his having built a church of white stone dedicated to Martin of Tours. Because of the building's unusual (i.e. Roman) construction the place was called the White House (candida casa). Just what the extent of Ninian's mission was may only be guessed. There is, however, an argument to be made for his having been bishop of a duly constituted Roman province necessitated by its remoteness. In any event, the presence of a bishop would tend to deny that Ninian's pastoral care of local Britons was in the nature of a missionary undertaking: it not being the contemporary practice of Rome to assign bishops to other than established centers of Christianity. Still, if there is truth to the suggestion of Ninian's devotion to Martin, we must be open to the idea that his vocation did admit of at least a partial missionary dimension: Martin having been a missionary bishop who incurred the wrath of authorities for his work among the peasants of his region; and such an attitude would be perfectly consistent with the tradition of Ninian laboring to convert the southern Picts. Of particular importance are the geographic proximity of Whithorn to the North of Ireland and the Irish tradition of many of her earliest monastics (including Enda of Aran and Finnian of Movilla) having studied at "Rosnat" (the Irish name for Candida Casa).

Still, we must not be misled by the bits and pieces of monastic popularity evident from 4th and 5th century Britain. Basically the Church there was Roman in organization, not communal: it was constructed and administered along lines of the imperial civil service, each bishop in complete charge of

his autonomous province or diocese and having recourse to
Rome in cases of dispute with his colleagues. That a prelate
might lead an ascetic existence did not, for the most part,
conflict with protocol as outlined by a series of councils
and the proclamations of the bishops of Rome.

In the shadowy first generation of the 5th century interest
in the Western Isles intensified. Rome's legions may have
abandoned Britian, but the Church had not; with ever-increasing secular responsibilities was included maintenance of contacts with outlying regions. The former province had, by the
reign of Celestine (422-32), given Rome cause for fear with
the Pelagian heresy. To combat this trouble Germanus, bishop of Auxerre, and Lupus, bishop of Troyes, were sent to Britain in 428-9. We have two contemporary references to St.Ger-
manus: 1) in the Anonymous Gaulish Chronicle for the year 433;
and, more important, 2) in the Epitoma Chronicon ("Summary of
Chronicles") of Prosper of Aquitaine for the year 429.The latter informs us that Germanus, sent at the suggestion of Deacon
Palladius by Pope Celestine as his representative, confounded
heretics corrupted by the Pelagian Agricola and directed the
Britons to the Catholic Faith (P&L, 248). There have been much
discussion and scholarly debate as to the details of Germanus'
trip: the identity of the principals responsible for the mission; the Church of Gaul's role in the procedure; whether or
not Germanus did indeed undertake a second mission to Britain
in or about 449. The question has been fully and masterfully
treated by N.K. Chadwick in P&L; perhaps the most readable account of Germanus' deeds in the matter may be found in Bede's
chapters 17-21 (Book I) of the Ecclesiastical History (a section derived almost exclusively from Constantius' Life of Germanus). Whatever contention there may be of the smaller view,
the larger picture is clear: the Western Isles, early in the
second generation of the 5th century,had become of greater fo-
focal importance to the continental Church and the Papacy. Nor
did Rome's concern over heresy in the West confine itself to
Britain. In the year 431, as noted by Prosper, Palladius (the
deacon who recommended Germanus?) is ordained by Pope Celestine and sent as the first bishop to the Scottos believing in
Christ. It should be understood that "Scot," well before the
5th century and for centuries thereafter, denotes "Irish" or
"Gael." To all intents and purposes, it would seem that Celestine's delegation marks the beginning of "official" Christianity in Ireland.

II   THE BEGINNINGS: PALLADIUS and PATRICK

Unfortunately our knowledge of Christianity's introduc-
tion into Ireland is little helped by the figure of Palladius. For that is what he is--a fleeting outline alluded
to as quoted from Prosper in but a few words. In fact we
cannot be certain that the Palladius who recommended Germanus is the same bishop sent to the "Scots." (Although the
equation appears more likely than not.) For such meager references are all we have relating to him. To be sure, later
Irish chroniclers, faced with this brief but seemingly irre-
futable documentation, felt compelled to note his existence
(as in the Annals of Ulster); and embellishments of his career were considered necessary by later hagiographers as well.
Nonetheless, his mission and accomplishments remain points of
contention.

The intriguing thing about Palladius is that his journey
to the "Scots" precedes by one year the date attributed in
the Irish Annals to the arrival of Ireland's traditional
apostle Patrick. In and of itself this circumstance would
not necessarily cause confusion were it not for a puzzling
passage in still another work by Prosper (Contra Collatorem,
"Against the Conferee," written as an anti-Pelagian tract in
response to John Cassian). Herein the work of Celestine is
mentioned with apparent reference to Palladius' appointment:
". . . and having ordained a bishop to the Scots, while en-
deavoring to preserve (studet servare) the Roman island Catholic, he also made the barbarian island Christian." It was accepted that Prosper meant "Ireland" by the "barbarous island"
until Carney's Thomas Davis Lecture of 1958 (reviewed and discussed in greater length by Carney on pp.49-52 of The Problem
of Patrick). According to this opinion, the "barbarian island" refers to the part of Britain beyond the Forth-Dumbar-
ton isthmus; i.e. the area outside the limits of Roman control. To support his contention, Carney offers a passage of
Tacitus' Agricola XXIII wherein the zone north of present-day
Glasgow and Edinburgh is described as "velut in aliam insula"
("as in another island"). Since it would be sometime near the
early 5th century that the "Scots" from Ireland established
themselves in this area, it follows that Palladius would have
been assigned to this flock rather than to those in Ireland.
Correct or not, this interpretation casts doubt on what had

been one of the rare sure points of Christianity's early history in Ireland.

The question of Patrick is more bemusing still. Someone consulting the Annals of Ulster will find the following recorded:

431 A.D. Celestine's mission to the Scots. (Doubtless Prosper's Chronicon served as the source of entry.)

432 A.D. Patrick's arrival in Ireland during the first year of the reign of Sixtus, bishop of Rome.

439 A.D. Secundus, Auxilius and Serninus are sent as bishops to aid Pat-·rick. (To which the Annals of Inishfallen add: "However, none but Patrick alone held the apostolate.")

441 A.D. Leo is ordained bishop of Rome and Patrick is approved in the Catholic Faith.

443 A.D. Patrick is flourishing in the passion (ardore) of faith and in the doctrine of Christ in our province.

444 A.D. Armagh is founded.

447, 459 and 468 A.D. are given as dates for the deaths, respectively, of Secundinus, Auxilius and Iserninus (as they are spelled this time).

457 A.D. The death of "Old Patrick" (senis Patricii) "as some say."

461 A.D. "Here some say the death of Patrick."

491 A.D. The death of Patrick (this time) archbishop. (The Annals of Inishfallen record Patrick's death in 496, in the 432nd year from the Lord's Passion.)

If the above were not confusing enough, the AU (467 A.D.) and the AI (468 A.D.) refer to the death of Benignus the bishop whom the AU call "the successor of Patrick"--implying,therefore, that Patrick died before 467-8.

The sketchy details, the evidently contradictory repetitions and the AU 457 mention of "Old Patrick" have set scholars to speculating not only as to the scope of Patrick's mission, but as to whether or not there might have been more than one individual of the same name laboring for Christ in Ireland in the 5th century.

Unfortunately for those in pursuit of the historical (or, perhaps, "real") Patrick, contemporary or near contemporary sources are of no help. (The Irish annals being compiled much after the 5th century.) Neither Prosper, nor Gildas (writing in the first half of the 6th century), nor Bede (writing in the early 8th century and leaving the most complete account of church history for our period in the Western Isles), nor Columbanus (late 6th--early 7th centuries) mentions the Apostle to the Irish. The first reference to Patrick outside of his own works is contained in a letter of Cummian, probably abbot of Durrow, written to Segene, abbot of Iona, in the 630's concerning the controversy over the dating of Easter (Chadwick, Saints, 130).

The "problem" of Patrick is not such simply for modern scholars; indeed, Patrick's earliest biographers, Muirchu and Tirechan (late 7th century) experienced confusion as to their subject (Carney, 34-9). Because of this and because such "biography" was composed in both the spirit of hagiography (wherein the intent is to inspire and edify rather than to report literal truth) and of controversy (in this case to advance the cause of Armagh as the religious "capital" of Ireland), this testimony has been the subject of erudite debate. Even before this century the matter was contested to the point that when in 1905 J.B. Bury lent his enormous prestige as a classical historian to the issue and published his Life of Patrick, "he created" (in John T. McNeill's words) "in his readers a gratified sense of finality" (p. 53). Bury, like Whitley Stokes before him, saw the 491 reference to Patrick's "death" as being an expansion made so as to have the saint's life conform to a Mosaic pattern: having the Apostle of Ireland live to an age like that of the Law Giver; and the dates of Patrick's coming and demise would correctly be 432 and 461 as noted in the annals. Time was to prove some scholars not gratified, Bury's solution un-final.

In 1942 T.F. O'Rahilly reopened the matter with a brilliant and unorthodox analysis and maintained that the confusion

of dates resulted from there having been "Two Patricks" working in Ireland--the earlier synonymous with none other than
Palladius who arrived in 431 and "who was called by the other
name 'Patrick'" according to Tirechan (discussion: Carney,
p. 39). Once the two identities have been sorted out (according to O'Rahilly) we have: 1) the "Old Patrick" (=Palladius)
who arrived in 431 and died in 461; and, 2) the "Second Patrick" or "Patrick the Briton"--the Patrick more familiar to us
and who left his Confession and a letter after arriving in approximately 462 and dying about 492.

Response and counter-response to theories on the "problem" have placed scholars in roughly one of two camps: the
self-styled "traditionalists" who are in general support of
the framework of Bury's contentions: Eoin MacNeill, John Ryan
and Ludwig Bieler; and those who largely follow O'Rahilly's
lead: James Carney and D.A. Binchy. What emerges is a spec-
trum of opinion as varied as controversial, extending from
a nigh-well total void as to the mission and significance
of Palladius, to a greater expansion of his presence in Ireland (as O'Rahilly sees it); from a view of Patrick (in "traditional terms") as having escaped to Gaul from Ireland as
a youth and (at some time or other) as having studied on the
Continent, to a rejection of his escape to Gaul, but acceptance of "part of his training in Gaul" (Carney, p.72), to
dismissal of any contact he might have had "with any Continental Church" as "entirely without foundation" (Dillon and
Chadwick, 176).

To scholar and interested lay reader alike the temptation
may be simply to throw up one's hands. This need not be necessary, even in terms of the above. As badly opposed as
the "schools" on the matter seem to be, a needed balance of
sorts has been struck: between the broad outline provided
by the Bury advocates and the innovative findings of those
who have followed O'Rahilly. As a result, the picture of a
more dynamic, living age of Patrick begins to emerge; the
gap between the "known" 5th century on the Continent and the
misty "unknown" of the 5th century in Ireland, as well as
the "void" separating Patrick's age from that of the 6th
century in Ireland, starts to narrow. Against the backdrop
of what now may appear to be Bury's somewhat credulous sce-
nario, we have the courage and intuitive genius of O'Rahilly's insights extended and refined by thorough and clear-
thinking scholars such as Carney whose reevaluations and new

discoveries continue to add flesh and blood to figures either previously cosmetized by fairytale or sketched in two-dimensional mechanics.

Carney's interpretation of the Patrician problem does not rely on a confusion of identities as such, but rather on the polemic exigencies of a later time. Crucial to an understanding of Patrick's biographers is their involvement in advancing the cause of Armagh as the overall seat of Ireland's ecclesiastical power. In fact the main works advancing this claim are contained in the circa 807 Book of Armagh: not merely those of Muirchu and Tirechan, but the Tripartite Life of Patrick and the Book of the Angel as well (Hughes, CEIS, appendix). For our purposes these represent the literary thrust of Armagh's argument: primacy in time and foundation by Patrick. To which may be added: proximity to the ancient center of power in Ulster--Emain Macha--the "premier seat of kingship" (Carney,23), prestige, politics and, perhaps, druidry as well. As Carney states: ". . .even before Christianity, Emain Machae may have been the religious capital of Ireland." In legend, history, culture and politics, Ireland from the 7th century onwards found herself gravitating to her ancient past and coming to terms with it. By exploiting such a force the Church of Armagh intended to make good its claims. To prove its point, history had to be adjusted.

Carney thoroughly reviews scholarship and evidence,including an additional piece to the puzzle in the form of an anonymous British chronicle (pp. 7ff.). From enormous complexities he concluded that Patrick's dates of arrival and death are: April 5, 456 and March 17, 493. The work prior to Patrick's coming and attributed to him are really the accomplishments of that Secundinus who came in 439 and who, called "Old Patrick" by the annals, died in 457. The founding of Armagh, listed as of 444, was achieved by Secundinus and a Roman mission. Confusion has arisen not because of the presence of two missionaries named Patrick, but out of a need "to depress Secundinus in the interest of Patrick" (p. 36). Since the latter was held to be the Apostle of Ireland, then he and he alone must have credit as such in full and proper order. Hence he is "approved" by Pope Leo in 441 and is thus in the country before the founding of Armagh and able to supplant Secundinus as its first bishop. Finally, Patrick's arrival is accorded the earliest date possible, 432, just after the incontrovertibly attested year 431 of the otherwise "mys-

terious" Palladius of whose career in Ireland nothing else
is known.

Whatever our judgment of such scholarship, it sheds light
on the machinations of living men, it brings an age alive.
Its chronology leads us nearer to the century following Patrick's: Carney, using much of O'Rahilly's arguments, points
out (14-7) that all those persons associated with the Patrician tradition are placed either in the second half of the
5th century or in the first half of the 6th. Not one seems
to have flourished in 432 (the AU date of Patrick's coming)
or shortly thereafter.

One must grant another point to those of Carney's persua-
sion.There is a close ring of similarity between protestations
in Patrick's writings and annal listings. At the beginning of
his Letter to Coroticus he declares himself to be a bishop,
accepting from God what he is; throughout his Confession runs
the theme of his unworthiness despite which God has directed
his steps to do the work He has commanded. It is as if the
AU 441 entry of Leo's "approval" of Patrick were an answer
countermanding criticism and dispelling any doubts. The same
might be said of the AU 443 listing that Patrick was "flourishing in the doctrine of Christ in our province"--a seeming
echo of assurance that the Apostle to the Irish was a true
believer in the efficacy of divine grace at a time when Pelagianism threatened the unity of the Church. And as to the
matter somewhat cryptically alluded to in the Confession 26,
3 (ed. Hanson)--that some of his elders (seniores) had cri-
ticized him and his "laborious episcopate" (laboriosum epis-
copatum)--this too evidently has a response in the Au entry
of 491 which records the death of Patrick, the archbishop.
As if the annalist wished to certify beyond question the legitimacy of Patrick's apostolate.

All supporting evidence consulted and scholarly speculation considered, the best witness for Patrick's career is
Patrick. We have two pieces unquestionably from his hand:
a letter, written in indignation to the troops of a nominal-
ly Christian British king (Coroticus) who had brutalized and
killed some of Patrick's recent converts; and his Confession,
apparently composed not merely as an acknowledgement (confes-
sio) of faith, but mainly as a defence of his person against
accusations leveled by elders (seniores) of his (so to speak)
mother church back in Britain. What the text of the latter
amounts to is a rapid, at times compact, at times run-on,often

vague summary of his life and justification of his mission.
Its references are frequently emotional, cryptic and ellip-
tical. Doubtless the details therein were clear to his contemporaries; for the modern reader they remain tantalizing-
ly challenging and, occasionally, impenetrable. Neither Patrick's faulty Latin nor his obviously mystical qualities of
personality helps clarify matters for us today.

An outline of Patrick's experiences follows. A young man,
born to a traditionally religious Christian family (his father Calpornius was a deacon and a minor local official; his
grandfather a priest--not unusual for the time) somewhere
along the western British coast, in or near a village (or
estate) called Bannavem Taberniae, had fallen in with bad
companions and "did not know the true God." Doubtless meaning he was not a good Christian, not that he was a pagan; for
he states that "we were not obedient to our priests" (ed. Hanson 1, 10). By God's wrath he, like thousands of others,was
taken captive and brought to the "end of the earth" (a theme
recalling the Acts of the Apostles 13, 47, and which Patrick
will continue to use with reference to Ireland).

From the beginning of the Confession we note the most per-
vasive element contributing to the mood of the work: events
and people (in particular Patrick) are guided by the ever-
present hand of God. In the opening judgment he passes on
his wayward youth, Patrick does more than simply condemn his
own lack of fidelity to God. His stigma extends to the British (i.e. Celtic speakers) in his region of pre-Saxon conquest. The theme of God's vengeance upon luke-warm and lapsed
Christians will reach its height in the 6th century with Gildas' account of Britain's destruction. For Patrick, even if
we could put aside his ordeals, Irish and Pictish assaults on
the remnants of Roman culture in his province would offer a
firm proof of divine disfavor toward its inhabitants.

Patrick sees God's will working within him--this is the
greatest support he draws upon in defending himself against
critics and in thanking his Saviour for changing his life.
Simply put: he is God's chosen for his mission, albeit an
unworthy nominee. In the Divinity's inscrutable way, Patrick was singled out, punished at the tender age of sixteen
with slavery and exile that he might come to know Him and do
His will by returning one day to the land of his tribulation
and bringing its people to Christ.

So at one with the Spirit does Patrick feel himself to be

14

that it is as if most of his steps through life have been charted by Holy Writ. Biblical passage and personal experience are constantly integrated as argument. Of the 62 sections of the Confession as established by Hanson, all but eleven contain some reference to or paraphrase of the Scriptures.

Patrick's declared intention (sec.6) is to make known to his "brothers and kinsmen" what sort of person he is that they may perceive the desire of his soul; for he knows the punishment due liars (sec. 7) and fears the day of judgment and reckoning (sec. 8). The scandal attached to the accusations leveled at Patrick caused him to think not only of how it might compromise his efforts in Ireland, but his reputation in Britain and the Church at large as well. However, his words have the cut of a double-edged blade: by implication, if the Lord promises punishment for the accused, if guilty, so will His wrath fall upon the accusers should they lie.

Accusation and criticism may cause anger and frustration of one kind; quite another is born of a feeling of inadequacy in the medium of defence. Concomitant with the waywardness of his youth was the saint's failure to acquire a proper Latin preparation. Insufficient education, we may project,would not be the only shortcoming he felt. It is at least possible that, given such fault, there was a tendency, if not open inclination on the part of some of his critics, to see this Apostle to the Irish as something less than a serious person: irregular, unreliable, rough and odd. We have evidence from Patrick's Letter to Coroticus (sec.16) of British contempt for the Irish, when, in lamenting his inability to save his converts from the ravages of so-called fellow-Christians such as the freebooter Coroticus, he states: Indignum est illis Hiberionaci sumus ("It is unworthy to them [the very fact that] we are Irish"). Whether or not Patrick, for the moment, chose to share spiritually in the nationality of his victimized flock, the message seems clear: just being Irish meant "barbarian" to the British. Even a pirate like Coroticus would share in this reflex. So here we have a formerly nonbelieving, troublesome youth who,although of fine family,never took the time to learn the language (Latin) of the Church, was fittingly punished by enslavement for six years among the barbarians (where he must have picked up some additional rough manners), was appointed to return as missionary to those bar-

barians,and now struggles to justify his backwoods methods and
questionable dealings in that very tongue.

Thoughts something like these might well lie beneath the
rather lengthy issue Patrick makes of his inadequacy, a theme
maintained for five sections of his address (secs. 9-13). Inadequacy and guilt: it is difficult to miss the regret experienced by one who has wasted the opportunity to learn correctly the ecclesiastical language and its facility needed to sus-
tain argument. So lacking (as his grammar shows) is his confidence that he describes what he puts forth as being "translated into a foreign tongue" <translata est in linguam ali-
enam>, sec. 9. Even allowing for exaggeration, his judgment
upon his education and consequent inability to express himself is harsh, perceived as they may be by the savor (saliva)
of his writing. With the fault of not reading more thoroughly as a youth, there is the factor of his captivity at an early age, both contributing to the woeful lack causing his shame.

Nonetheless, there is in Patrick the obligation to speak
out and defend himself. He bolsters his need with a quota-
tion from Isaiah 32, 4 that "stuttering tongues shall quickly
learn to speak peace" (sec. 11), and from Paul (II Corinthi-
ans 3, 2-3) that "we are. . . a letter of Christ for the sake
of salvation unto the ends of the earth," if not eloquent,
"written in your hearts--not in ink--in the Spirit of the
living God," for "even the life of the rustic is created by
the Most High" (Sirach 7, 16).

It is God who uplifted one who was so low ("like a stone
lying in mud," sec. 12), raising him for His purposes. For
this reason must Patrick speak aloud, here and in the hereafter, in gratitude for blessings so great that the mind of
men (mens hominum) cannot appraise them. The combination of
confidence and indignation causes him at this point (sec. 13)
to challenge his learned judges, superior though they be in
the ways of this world. Somewhat sarcastically he apostro-
phizes his "learned lords of clever rhetoric" (domini cati
rhetorici; see: Hanson, 82-3, n.4 and Carney, 98 for the textual question) that they might learn Who it was that inspired
him, one abominable to this world, to faithfully perform good
for the people God's charity has brought him to.

The double irony is not lost. What better way to fulfill
the divine plan than that a wayward, guilty ignoramus work out
his redemption by serving the very people which held him captive, and that through the example of this calling the learn-

ed learn the ways of God and not men!

Recounting at last his captivity's most significant aspects (starting with sec. 16), Patrick offers a cursory image of a boy who had much lonely time to himself in tending his master's flocks. As the love of God and His fear came over him so did his faith grow, his spirit move; wherever he was, in whatever weather, he would pray, perhaps a hundred times by day and as much by night; he felt no pain or sloth, for the spirit burned within. It was from this state of shock, new-found reverence and resilience that after six years of servitude the new man emerged.

One night, in his sleep, he heard a voice telling him that he would soon return to his homeland (sec. 17); and a little later that his boat was ready, not nearby but at a distance of some two hundred thousand paces (i.e. 200 Roman miles-- perhaps 150 English miles), where he had never been and where he knew no one. The revelation was oracular; Patrick uses the word <responsum> to describe it, a term honored by such implication in both Testaments and in pagan antiquity (Hanson, 86, n.2). Right after, he took to flight, leaving his captor of six years; and strengthened by the power of God (in virtute Dei), who also guided the way, he feared nothing until he came upon the boat. From the time of Patrick's sleep the entire affair is like a dream-sequence. Surely the incidental details have been omitted as unimportant. What Patrick has done with his narrative is sacrifice accuracy to effect. He is writing in the heat of emotion and consequently arranges events and details according to drama. At this point he is literally swept along by divine guidance--nothing else matters; nothing could bar the realization of God's will.

Suddenly he has arrived (sec. 18). But where? We do not know. Nor, evidently, does it matter to Patrick. Perhaps he, at least when he first got there, did not know himself. He simply came to the place where he was guided, he might say. Critics have debated, in terms of proximity to Britain and distance whence he came (the 200 Roman miles), as to his place of servitude and point of departure (Carney, passim; Hanson, 33ff.). It is unlikely that any one locus for each will ever have universal scholarly acceptance. Probably, given the distance traversed, Ireland's small area and Patrick's ultimate destination (somewhere in Britain) he set out from the west and eventually found passage along the east coast.

The boat had already been moved from its place (de loco

suo; see: Hanson, 89, n.1) and Patrick spoke with "them" about sailing with them. "They" being the members of the crew. What was said about Patrick's escape applies here as well. At first impression, not a second is wasted: if we follow his recounting literally, no sooner does he arrive than we see his escape-vessel set to depart. We learn, however, after the captain has refused him passage, that there must have been some recent stop-off point for Patrick, because he starts to move away from the ship's company to return to the hut (tegoriolum) where he had been staying. Had he received lodging from some nearby cotter;or had he simply held up in an abandoned shack? It is impossible to tell. One thing we do see from this de-detail, apart from the obvious fact that he did not make the journey in one non-stop effort: this sort of minutia, of which there must have been dozens or even hundreds, is irrelevant to the narrator and, quite possibly, already familiar to the most important of his readers/listeners.

While leaving after the refusal Patrick prays; and before he is finished he hears one of the crew call him to return and to promise friendship with them in whatever way he choose. Patrick had declined (we now learn) the pagan practice of sucking their breasts as a sign of loyalty. This we may deduce, was most probably the cause of the captain's denying him passage. Once again, as the sequence of prayer-then-change-of-heart by the crew indicates,God's will has intervened and Patrick is allowed to sail.

The next four sections, compact and elliptic in style, recount the remainder of his experience before returning home. Many of the details have been debated in the arena of scholarly contention; much will never be resolved. The reader will profit by consulting the opinions of Bury, Bieler, Carney and Hanson,among others. We will endeavor to make consistent sense out of the sometimes cryptic style and allusions of the narrator.

After three days the company touched land. They were to travel twenty-eight days through uninhabited country (sec. 19). From all indications, it would be Britain they reached (Carney, 65ff.); and it seems that, given Patrick's statement in section 21 ("the sixtieth night the Lord delivered me from their hands,"), he considered himself a prisoner of the ship's company--therefore making these seafarers more pirates than merchants. In fact they may very well have been of the sort which had kidnapped him from his home--a detail consistent

with the historical evidence of Irish raiders of the time exploiting the west coast of Britain (Carney, 67).

Eventually the company runs out of food and the captain
challenges Patrick to the effect that if his God is so great,
why does he not pray to Him for help. To which Patrick an-
swers that they should convert to Him for Whom nothing is impossible, so that He send them food in abundance. And, as if
in immediate demonstration of the power of faith, a herd of
(wild) pigs appears which provided food for the starving men
to gorge and refresh themselves for two days before continuing their march.

There is a still-vexing textual question involving line
14 of section 19 (Hanson's edition): whether to read ⟨carnes⟩
("meat"--i.e. the pigs' flesh) or ⟨canes⟩ ("dogs"--i.e. wolf-
hounds which would, then, form part of the traders' wares).
Increasingly scholars have come to accept the reading "carnes"
(plural of "meat") and to reject the idea of hounds (nowhere
else referred to) refreshing themselves on the flesh provided.
Carney (pp. 75ff.) and Hanson (p.92, n. 1) discuss the problem
in enlightening detail, both accepting ⟨carnes⟩ as the correct
version, thus allowing the passage as describing the men re-
storing themselves on the meat "because many (i.e. men) had
been overcome (with hunger) and abandoned half-alive by the
roadside."

The drama of section 19 continues, for the freebooters gave
thanks to God, and Patrick himself was honored but, nonetheless,
endangered by a pagan act. It seems that some wild honey had
been found and some of it offered to Patrick. Apparently he
was on the verge of taking it when told: Immolaticum est ("It
has been offered"). According to Carney (p.78 and n. 1) such
would involve the custom of pouring a libation to the "otherworld folk" before imbibing. Fortunately, we are told, Patrick
did not taste any. As Carney has shown, refusal underscores
Patrick's fidelity to the reproach of Saint Paul (I Corin. 10,
28): Si quis autem dixerit: Hoc immolatum est idolis, nolite
manducare ("But if anyone should say to you,'This has been offered in sacrifice to idols,' do not eat it . . ."). To which
we might add, from the same letter, in reference to Moses' people all partaking of the same spiritual food and drink: Sed
non in pluribus eorum beneplacitum est Deo; nam prostrati sunt
in deserto (vs.5)--"But most of them were not pleasing to God;
for they lay prostrate in the desert." In retrospect, the el-
derly bishop sees himself as a young man of about twenty-two

walking in the ways of Moses and Paul.

That very night another temptation came to him (increasingly shown as a man of vision) in his sleep (sec.20). The devil fell upon him like an enormous rock and he suddenly cried out "Heliam." Why and how he should do so he does not say. But as he did he saw the sun rise in the heavens and shine upon him, thus scattering all weight from him. This he believed came about from Christ Who cried out in his behalf (pro me; see: Carney, 82-3; Hanson, 94, n. 1). Seemingly the pagan practice of the previous section set in motion an association in the mind of the narrator: just as the young Patrick came so so close to tasting of a pagan offering, then, in his sleep (the time when all his visions seem to come upon him), because of the devil's efforts, he is dangerously near to confusing Christ (Whom he will later call <solem verum Christum>--"the true sun Christ," sec.60) with the object of the pagan suncult, but is saved by Him speaking in him (Hanson, 93, n. 6).

At the beginning of section 21 there is a somewhat confusing reference to another occasion of Patrick's being captive "many years later" (post annos multos adhuc). This seems to recall an ordeal mentioned later on in sections 37 and 52 (if, indeed, they were the same incidents)--in the former he describes himself, like Paul in II Timothy 2,9, as being in chains. Why he chooses to insert such now may escape the reader except as an association with the fact that at this point, in the captivity of raiders, he hears another divine pronouncement (responsum divinum) declare that he will stay two months in their company. Which came about; and he was delivered. The idea would be that then, as later, God led his steps, imprisoning and freeing him according to His will.

The Lord continued to provide sustenance and good weather until the tenth day (presumably after coming upon the swine) when, after twenty-eight days of wandering, and at the end of their food, they met other humans (sec. 22).

Patrick's recounting of his escape from Ireland ends abruptly there; in fact, we are not told (as we were not informof how he left the place of his captivity) just how he managed to get away from the ship's crew. With section 23 we emerge into another time--a few years later when he is back in Britain with his relatives. At this point he will speak of his vocation, his experiences as a missionary, his trust in God--all part of his answer to those charges (whatever their details) prompting his personal defence.

20

It might be best to summarize the rest of his Confession in terms of its themes so as to stress the essentials of his argument and the emotional nature of its basis. As Kathleen Hughes (CEIS, 34-5) has succinctly stated, two objections to Patrick by his superiors (seniores) were his being a sinner and an unlearned man--both of which he admits. We have seen him granting the latter; the former is somewhat more complex. It involves the dredging up, by a friend in whom he had confided, of something he had done when barely fifteen years of age. The very friend who seems to have at one time defended him and to have announced his forthcoming appointment as bishop (sec. 32). The idea of making capital of an incident which took place before even his captivity,conversion and ordination as deacon is described as a thirty-year-old pretext (occasionem, sec. 27)--presumably, that is, thirty years after he began his missionary work with the Irish. Patrick does not deny the allegation (whatever it means); but, by implication, it was a different person, a boy, a youngster as yet untouched by the hand of God who was guilty. The Patrick now accused is the man who has received God's call, a gift of loving Him to the point of leaving all for His sake (sec. 36). In fact, the very day he was censured (reprobatus) he had a night vision (vidi in visu noctis, sec. 29; just as the same phrase is used in sec.23 to describe his call to Ireland in still another such experience), wherein he saw placed before his face something written which dishonored him and he heard a divine pronouncement (again: responsum divinum): "To Our displeasure We have seen the face of the one designated, name laid bare" (Hanson, 103, n.3: a discussion of the various readings of the text at this point). And Patrick stresses that the voice spoke in terms of "We," not "you." Thus recalling to him the words of Zacharia 2, 12: "Who touches you it is as if he touches the pupil of My eye." Patrick's counter, then, to charges of sin, is that of election. All of his references to visions of various sorts--his call to escape, his protection from the devil, the promise that he would remain with the brigands for two months, the "voice of the Irish" (as described in sec.23) that he "walk once again" among them, as well as fortuitous responses to prayers and moments of protection in times of danger-- are for Patrick proof of divine approval.

The most serious allegation was evidently of more contemporary import. Corruption. Corruption involving personal profit and doubtless made credible by the irregular practices of

Patrick's mission. He leads into his defence on this issue by
expressing gratitude to God for never having gotten very angry
with his foolishness (sec. 46). He addresses those in Britain
who know he has been sincere and loyal since youth (sec. 48).
In effect, he has never cheated any of those among whom he labors, lest there be a reaction against them or that God's name
be blasphemed because of him. In fact,he states, he has arous-
ed the ire of some of his female converts by giving back valu-
ables they (possibly following some pagan Irish custom) had
thrown on his altar. This he has done to be above reproach,
especially to non-believers. Patrick makes a strong case for
his honesty: in asking if he ever hoped for so much as a cop-
per coin from·any of the thousands he baptized;in stating that
he freely distributed the ministries of his ordained clerics
(in this case quite possibly contrary to Gaulish practice);
and in offering to repay if he so much as asked anyone of them
for the price of shoes (sec. 50). On the contrary, in sections
51-3 we learn that it is he who has spent for those who hear
him--that he might be admitted there where no one had ever
gone before to spread the faith. In fact, he had offered, at
times, gifts to kings; had been arrested and come near death.
He had even paid out no less than the price of fifteen men to
judges in the places he visited so that "you might enjoy me
and I you in God" (sec. 53). (This seemingly a reference to
purchasing fellow Christians out of slavery;as he would doubtless have liked to have done for the victims of Coroticus,
Letter, sec. 14--and, just possibly, to the need to compensate
families whose members had become clergy, Confession, sec.52.)
   The crux of the problem apparently involved what has been
suggested in our first chapter: the Roman concept of a bishop (even for those living in the backwater of Britain) would
have been that of a stable, dignified administrator who gov-
erned his see from a central place and established his authority through a network of subordinate churches. Patrick had
none of this to work with. No central authority. Only local
territories jealously commanded by warlords living (as far as
we can tell) by standards of Iron Age heroics. As Kathleen
Hughes remarks (CEIS, 35): "Patrick himself was constantly on
the move, and he travelled with a retinue suited to his rank."
This is what Patrick was describing when he mentioned the "pay
<mercedem> I gave to the kings' sons who travel with me." From
the beginning he (who, we must not forget, knew Irish customs as his seniores did not) both acclimated and accommodated

himself to the society he had to deal with. Warlords and their
people must be approached;they will not,at first, come to you.
And, when you do approach them, it must be on their terms: you
must bring an offering; you must come honorably, in dignity,if
you would honor them so that they might honor you;you must exchange gifts; if you possess knowledge (and Patrick was literate), you must teach their sons. Patrick's problem was not unlike that of Martin of Tours who achieved a breakthrough on
the Continent: he chose to bring the Faith to one largely ne-
glected class, the backwoodsman, the peasant. It is no mistake
that the word for "pagan" <paganus> originally meant "country-
man."

From Patrick's own words, then, we have the best insight
as to not only his reactions and personality, but the conditions under which he labored--problems originating both from
within his "parish" and the land of his birth. To outsiders
he was controversial, ignorant, erratic, "irregular" in his
ministry. From his point of view, his work was God-appointed
and necessarily adapted in style to the unusual circumstances
of dealing with an untamed, rural, warrior-oriented society.
As the modern observer views it, Patrick's see was basically
Roman in character--he was answerable to his superiors in Britain from whom he doubtless received financial support--but
it was also somewhat fluid in nature, given the required itinerant features of his efforts. (Such being obliged not only
by dint of Irish geography, but by force of Irish custom as
well.) There was apparently a monastic element in the mode of
his church: in both his Confession (sec. 41) and Letter (sec.
12) he speaks of the "monks and virgins of Christ." Whether
he established any sort of dwellings actually separated from
society, and to what degree, one may only speculate. Surely
Patrick himself, like many a great monastic before and after
him, would have found little time apart from the world. Still,
this would not disqualify from monasticism the likes of Martin of Tours,Columba, Columban, Boniface, Bernard of Clairvaux
and scores of others required by circumstance and need to deal
with man in a world of mammon.

We know really nothing of his preparation for his task.
It has been argued that he learned his Latin in Gaul (Christine Mohrmann, LSP); but it has been shown by the studies of
Bieler, Green and Jackson that a Latin-speaking community did
exist in 5th-century Britain. Which would explain, among
other things, some of the archaic features of Patrick's Latin.

Carney (p.72) believes that "we may confidently say that he received part of his [monastic] training in Gaul," and favors the tradition that places such preparation at Lerina, the community founded by Honoratus off the coast of the Provence. Carney points out that Patrick expresses the desire (Confession, sec. 43) to visit his "brothers in Gaul and see the face of the saints of my Lord." However, one might just as well interpret this as indicative of nostalgia inspired by old aspirations, images created in the mind of someone raised and trained to idealize the origin of so much that characterizes the insular Church: Gaul, land of Martin of Tours. Nora Chadwick, correctly recalling the aims of later generations and herself somewhat prone to detect politics, discounts any veracity to the tradition of Patrick's continental connections, placing them in the same light as other fancies passed on to us by his later biographers Muirchu and Tirechan (both late 7th century) writing in the interests of the Church of Armagh (see: D&C,183-4). Indeed, there is no reason why Patrick might not have gotten much of his Latin training from his father or from an associate of his ecclesiastical family.

On the personal level, there is much in Patrick that will be observed in Irish monastics. What we have in him is a humble but righteous man who knows himself to be chosen (albeit unworthy of such) by God; a man conscience-stricken for having squandered much of his youth (thus not acquiring the proper education),admittedly slow to answer the call within (sec.46), but grateful for having been laid low and thus uplifted by a merciful Saviour. In his description of divine revelation there is an unmistakable genuineness which strikes the modern ear: his experiences are not molded in the form conventional to hagiography (Hanson, 49). He is also a man of kindness, fidelity and generosity: fearful for his flock (particularly the women who are either mistreated by unsympathetic families or brutalized by slavetraders like Coroticus), totally devoted to his calling, capable of giving his all to redeem the enslaved or to pay compensation for those who have rejected paganism. A mystic, bolstered by the conviction of his work in God and living emotionally in the immanence of biblical prophecy, he is fearless while castigating the inhumanity of Coroticus and in reproving the unfair smugness of his superiors and colleagues in Britain who, although perhaps justified in questioning his methods, surely had no gauge for evaluating the need for unique measures in unique circumstances. Desirous of a better life and seeing martyrdom as the surest way to attain it, such a man would not be undone by the persecutions of this world; for whereas lesser men are caused by such to break, for him they were the source of abiding strength.

III   PATRICK'S PUZZLING CENTURY

Whatever dates we assign Patrick's mission, it is during or very near the time of his efforts that the Roman Empire experienced the ignominy of collapse. Patrick's century was that of Alaric the Visigoth (Rome sacked in 410), the Vandalic (seizure of North Africa (Carthage taken in 439), the invasion of Attila's Huns (routed on the Catalaunian Plains in 451), and the deposal of the last "official" Roman Emperor Romulus Augustulus by Odovacar the Herulian (476). Lamenting the events of 410, Jerome (who would not live to witness Rome's ensuing humiliations) wrote: "Now is held captive the city which once held captive the world."

Nor was Britain, bereft of Rome's legions, free from turmoil. About mid-century the island suffered the establishment of Angles and Saxons within its eastern shores. The details are sketchy and our knowledge depends mostly on accounts given a century later by Gildas. A major portion of British failure to effectively resist and eventually overcome the Germanic invasions (which took place over generations) can doubtless be attributed to inability or unwillingness to transcend fragmented interests and organize a sufficient federated counterattack. Infighting, misbegotten ambition, shortsighted gain seem to have had the upper hand. Tradition has it that the Britons, devastated by plague and weakened by a two-pronged attack of Picts on the north and "Scots" on the west, felt obliged to enlist the services of German mercenaries led by Hengist and Horsa--quasi-legendary figures whose great-great grandfather is listed in Bede I, xv as none other than (here demythologized) Wotan. Crucial to the tragedy of post-Roman Britain is a sense of ebb and flow of native resistance, the identity of the Cymric warlord Arthur (not mentioned by Gildas or Bede), and the locale and scope of the battle of Mount Badon (circa 500?)--in effect the Briton's last great triumph over their antagonists. Contention as to details aside, by the end of the 6th century the most formidable power in Britain was Anglo-Saxon.

Continental and insular strife did considerably inhibit travel and communications. But not nearly so much as once assumed. Britain and the Continent were, indeed, troubled during the 5th and 6th centuries,even devastated, but by no means experienced interdiction of traffic. As we have seen, concern over the Pelagian "infection" in Britain as well as among the Irish would continue throughout this period and into the 7th century. Effective counter-measures could not have been implemented without maintenance of sufficient contacts throughout the Church. And again, it is the considered opinion of Nora K. Chadwick (Age of the Saints, 22ff.) that, while rejecting Patrick's alleged continental education as an invention of a later age, both his Confession and Letter, for all the poverty of grammar, reflect in convention, style and phrasing an essential cultural unity with and awareness of the Church of Gaul.

Patrick's century was,then,a period of turmoil and destruction; but not accurately to be described as one of stagnation. Violence is its own sort of activity;conflict affords occasion of response and new creation. So it was for the Western Isles, particularly Ireland. So long a mysterious backwater at the edge of empire, her internal forces rippled outward and formed a tangent with the flood of history.

The North of Ireland in the 5th century shows the Ui Neill dynastic families (tracing their ancestry to Niall Noigiallach --Neil of the Nine Hostages) establishing themselves as the dominant force in a large arc of territory extending from northern Connacht in the west,across Ulster in the north and penetrating southeastward into Leinster. The sequence of events leading to this emerging hegemony is obscure and, perhaps, in many details untraceable (see: Mac Niocaill, pp. 8ff.). Beyond dispute are the following: 1) the Ulaid (whose name is at the origin of "Ulster"), chiefly the Dal Riata, were being pressured into an overseas search for land by the encirclement of hostile groups; 2) the Lagin (whose name is at the origin of "Leinster") were engaged in what was to be a protracted and losing struggle to maintain control of the Tara dynasty. Still farther south, the 5th century reveals the solidifying in east Munster of Eoganacht control of Cashel through the aid of the Deisi, a people expelled from Tara in the 3rd century by the legendary Cormac Mac Airt. Each of these displacements was to exert some influence on Irish contact with the outside world. (See: Map II)

The shortest route between Britain and Ireland leads from Antrim to Argyll. It was also the most natural for that remnant of the Ulaid, the Dal Riata, with its land greatly reduced and its back to the sea. The founding of Scottish Dal Riata (begun, perhaps, in the early 5th century) is the most important among Irish settlements in Britain both in terms of length of time and historical significance. Its place in Irish monasticism will require detailed discussion in a later chapter. For the present suffice it to say that from this area in south-west Scotland will come the impetus for the conversion and civilizing of the highlands, the first lasting Christianizing of the Anglo-Saxons, and, at a time beyond the scope of this study, the formation of the kingdom of Scotland. To the south-east of Argyll, and not much farther from Ireland, lies the area of Galloway--traditionally the place of Ninian's church--facing the modern counties of Antrim and Down.Here a study of place-names describing terrain and geography has revealed what Charles Thomas (ECT, 55-7) calls a "surprising... intense localized concentration" indicating an early Irish colony (of the 6th century?) which has no historical record. It may not be too highly speculative, if one scans the relative geographical positions of Galloway and eastern Ulster, to suggest--given the precarious straits of the Ulaid in the 5th and 6th centuries--that the Galloway settlement might be of Dal Fiatach origin (i.e. from east Down; see: O'Rahilly, EIHM, 346ff.). The latter people having, at that time, easiest access to the region of the Mull. Below Galloway, the Isle of Man is doubtless part of the Irish sphere from a time roughly contemporary with the settlements in Scotland. In north Wales, Caernarvonshire contains what appear to be farmhouse groups of typical Irish origin, tradition ascribing the name of the Llyn peninsula to the Lagin, whose homeland is directly across the Irish Sea (Thomas, 58ff.).

It is with the southern Welsh peninsula, known as Demetia in Roman times and Dyfed today, that we come to the area of most lasting Irish influence outside of Scotland. Here large numbers of the Deisi migrated under the leadership of Eochaid Allmuir (Eochaid "Beyond the Sea"). It has been stated that Dyfed is most convincing for the numerous ogham inscriptions (dedications incised in the borders of upright stones and composed of a linear system based on the Roman alphabet); one of the most interesting of which (c. 550) gives the Irish form (Votecorigas) of a name otherwise rendered as "Voteporigis" (the British version) in Roman letters. (In certain linguistic environments Gaelic dialects have "c" while Cymric dialects of Celtic show the letter "p.")

Finally, the farthest south-western British area,Cornwall: the eastern half, bordering Devon, reveals late 5th-century ogham inscriptions which in Charles Thomas' estimation attests an Irish colony having relations with its contemporaries in south Wales and in Ireland; western Cornwall has yielded late 6th-century pottery so similar to Ulster types of early Christian times that, according to Thomas (p. 65), "we can only regard them as due to Irish settlers." (Map III)

The movement of Irish to Britain is but one direction taken by the course of events bringing Gaels into ever-increasing contact with the outside world. It is difficult to speculate what its impact might have been were it the only one, for it is feasible that Irish numbers in western Britain at the time might well have equalled or even surpassed those of the Germanic invaders in the east. (Thomas, 66.)

History has its own Newtonian factor: action inevitably summons reaction. While there were numerous Irish incursions into Britain, so also were there British interests in the direction of Ireland. Patrick is a prime example of a long and persistent tradition--both legendary and factual--of British missionary efforts and influences in the westmost island. While his Confession gives testimony of his own captivity (the aim and result of who-knows-how-many such sorties by Gaelic freebooters),his Letter to Coroticus informs us that the British too were taking their toll in slaves from the Irish. His writings refer to what seems to be a substantial British population in Ireland: there for how long and as a result of what circumstances, one can only surmise. Whatever they may have been,one thing is unmistakable: traffic across the North Channel and the Irish Sea must have been significant and hazardous, for many reasons, and not interdicted for lack of courage or enterprise.

We have already seen that Patrick, for all his orthodoxy, was compelled to work in unique circumstances. We have also noted a remark in his Letter which implied British contempt for the Irish. An ambivalent attitude toward a people considered uncivilized by another which has been exposed to Christianity and Roman culture had to be shared by Patrick himself-- why else would he judge working for the conversion of Gaelic souls so great a sacrifice as to merit salvation? Or, put a different way: do not missionaries almost by definition look upon their charges as rather less-than-civilized children who must be brought to abandon their barbarous ways? There is so often involved an element of benign condescension which makes possible in the missionary his love for the very people which persists in back-sliding, forgets its proper gratitude, and is a constant source of sorrow for its long-suffering patron.

Whatever the finer points of British influence on early Irish Christianity and whoever the saints engaged in the undertaking may have been, the tradition of learning passing from western Britain to Ireland remained strong. It was to become a convention (perhaps literary as well as factual) for leading figures of early Irish monasticism to study in Britain: individuals no less than Finnian of Clonard and Brendan of Clonfert reportedly sharing in the experience. The most convincing evidence for such influence is found in Latin loan-words (mostly ecclesiastical) passing into Archaic Irish (as observed in manuscripts from the early 8th century). This terminology entered the Irish language, not with the purest Latin pronunciation, but with Brythonic articulation. Thus the word in Latin (borrowed from Greek) for "priest"--presbyter--could not possibly become Old Irish <cruimther> had it not been taken into Old Irish by way of a British-Latin form something like <*premiter> (Jackson, LHEB, 126). The seemingly odd change in the initial "p" sound should be explained. As stated above, the Gaelic language in its history has shown a peculiar treatment of the "p" sound elsewhere so prevalent in the Indo-European languages. To greatly simplify the matter: in early Archaic Irish as we know it "p" did not exist, and so was changed initially, in foreign words coming into Irish, to a palatal sound "c." Perhaps the most interesting example of this mutation occurs in the name of Patrick himself. Patricius was eventually to become Padrig (spelled Patric in Old Irish), but its earliest form is Cothriche--taken into the language at a very early stage of the Christian period. Such phenomena speak eloquently for the fact that the Irish did learn to pronounce Latin as their British teachers spoke it.

Nor were Britain's west and Ireland's east unique in their dynamism. It has been termed "reasonable" to conjecture the flight of Britons before the Germanic invaders during the age of Patrick (Kenney, 171). Gaul too, at the time of the Goths, Huns and Suevi, could, given the unimpeded passage from France to Ireland, be counted on for its levy of refugees. And it is in the second half of the 5th century that massive migration, continuing throughout the 6th century, was begun from Cornwall to Brittany.One might reason that since it was presumably preferable to be in western France rather than in south-west Britain for so many people, there must have been rather more security in certain areas of the Continent than in some regions of Britain. There is also evidence of lines of communication (and indeed the probability of refugee passage) into southern Ireland from the Aquitaine, and the Mediterranean, including North Africa and the Near East. (Consult: Thomas, 86-8, for pottery distribution in Ireland and Britain; Kenney, 142, on the Leyden Glossary; Chadwick, 50-8). To western Britain, then on to Ireland,or to southern Ireland directly,would come, therefore,in varying degrees and numbers,men of learning,their books, their ideas, their art, their rituals,tales of the desert, traditions of the Fathers, their sayings, wisdom,and yes, love of the ascetic life. In the next century strong lines of contact would be established between Ireland and Galicia, and ultimately the Visigothic Kingdom of Spain (converted to Catholicism after the 3rd Council of Toledo in 589; see: Deanesly, HEME, 93ff.).

What emerges gradually and in subsequent generations is a clearer focus on Ireland as a non-dominating, but most important element in a network of so-called Celtic Church entities. Not "Celtic Church" as a separate creed or profession, but as a unique manifestation, culturally and ideally,of a heretofore peripheral people's assimilation of a new message, a vision of hope, learning and humanity which it made its own and which it considers its mandate to share as spiritual food with whoever will partake. Ireland, traditionally the most archaic of Celtic nations,member of a once vast,feared and nearly exterminated race,will by force of geography and time, find its moment has come, not when it can bring Rome to its knees (as once the Gauls dreamt), or when its numbers can withstand Germanic onslaught, but when her warrior sons will fight for Christ, conquer the ignorance of Wotan's children, and brave the frontier that Rome lost.

Thus far our observations have been general, as our information commands. It has been suggested that movement from the time of Patrick into the 6th century conveys a feeling of losing direction--somehow the gap seems unbridgeable (Chadwick, 61). It is surely one of the more difficult links for the historian to reforge;and up to now we have only hinted at distin-

guishing Patrick's mission from that in any other part of Ireland. We did see in the preceding chapter the argument advanced by those of the O'Rahilly-Carney persuasion that history
has been "adjusted" to accommodate (for reasons political and
otherwise) the Patrician legend. We noticed the intriguing,
puzzling names Secundinus, Auxilius and Iserninus--somehow
connected with the Patron. It should be noted that the names
of the first two have been preserved in Meath and Kildare,
respectively, in the foundations Dunshaughlin (Domnach Sech-
naill) and Killashee (Cell Ausaile) (see: Mac Niocaill, 23-4).
The names Auxilius and Iserninus also appear after Patrick's
in the extraordinary so-called First Synod of Patrick--what
has been termed a circular letter of instructions or guidelines for church organization and conduct. Ludwig Bieler
(Penitentials, p.2) would date this document from the early
days of the Church in Ireland, circa 457 (arrived at from the
annalistic date of Auxilius' death); Kathleen Hughes (CEIS,
44-9 & ECI, 68-71), basing her views on the degree of organization and the relation of church to society implicit in the
decree, has opted for the mid-6th century. The importance of
the document for us at this point is two-fold: be the text of
the mid-5th or mid-6th century, it shows that the church first
constituted in Ireland was certainly "Roman" in character,
therefore in conformity with the concepts of episcopal autonomy; secondly,if there be any truth to the arguments of those,
like Carney,who perceive beneath the surface of available evidence indication of the suppression of Secundinus' accomplishments to the advantage of Patrick for the sake of late-date
legend-building,the First Synod may be another example of it:
here we have not the First Synod of the Bishops Secundinus,
Auxilius and Iserninus, but of Patrick et alii. We might ask
what happened to Secundinus. The Annals of Ulster give his
obituary as in 447; but we have already reviewed the confusion
involved therein. Declaring whether or not Patrick's name is
legitimately assigned to the First Synod would seem, at this
stage of available evidence,to require an individual research-
er's confession of faith.

Given the accessibility of southern Ireland from the Continent, it is not surprising to note that the lower portion
of the island has its own tradition of missionaries who pre-
ceded Patrick. Chief among them are: Declan of Ardmore (patron
of the Deisi in Ireland whose kindred invaded Dyfed); Ailbe
of Emly; Ciaran of Saigir; and Abban of Moyarney (see: Kenney,

309ff. for discussions of texts). (Map IV.) As with all Lives
of the Saints contained in the great manuscript collections
(Kilkenniensis,Insulensis and Salmanticensis;see: Hughes, ECI,
220-1; Plummer, VSH,ix-xxiii), the form in which we have these
early saints' Vitae was finalized centuries after they lived.
Nonetheless, despite legendary material incorporated therein
along with remnants of magic and superstition from the pre-
Christian past, the thread of evidence most pertinent to our
interests is the common rationalization of their status, the
"regularizing" of their relationship to the prestige of Patrick. Each of the above (and Ibar of Beggary Island of whom no
Life survives, but who is clearly shown in the Lives of the
others as the strongest opponent of Patrick's ecclesiastical
overlordship) is depicted as an earlier contemporary of the
Patron and as someone who finally, after hesitation, accepts
his primacy. It has been suggested that the idea of resist-
ing Patrick's authority might well have been an invention of
a post-Patrician age in which Munster sought to maintain independence from Armagh. Kenney (pp. 310-11) has convincingly
pointed out that,on the contrary,the whole tendency of later
hagiography was to reconcile such material with the Patrick-
legend, rather than deviate therefrom. Therefore, the somewhat dissident element present in these Lives—much of it
seemingly quite early in origin—would tend to point up an
area of missionary activity independent of Patrick, and add
one more piece to the tantalizing picture-puzzle of ancient
Christian Ireland.

IV   THE EMERGING IRISH ORDER

Our evidence is scant, to say the least, for trying to account for the changes occurring between the church Patrick labored to establish and the monastic institutions which domin-
ate the Irish scene from the end of the 6th century on. The
earliest document implicitly defining the Church's attitude
in Ireland is the so-called First Synod of Patrick noted in
the last chapter (Bieler, Penitentials, 54-9). In it we do not
detect the voice of a triumphant Christianity in a position to
terminate pre-Christian ways;rather it is one (as Hughes says,
CEIS,45) "still struggling against a pagan environment." Thus
the Ireland of the mid-6th century shows the converted population as a definite minority. A minority enjoined, to some de-

32

gree at least, to distance itself from the ways of the majority. Thus, for example, according to article 21, Christians
are to seek redress not in court (in iudicium), but in the
Church; failure to do so would meet with the penalty of being
estranged (alienus), presumably from the Christian community.
Alms are not to be accepted from either pagans (a gentibus)
or excommunicants (articles 12 & 13). All members of the clergy are instructed to adopt the Roman manner of dress and shorn
hair;their wives are to be veiled. Otherwise they shall be re-
moved from the Church (article 6). Terse regulations are prescribed as to ecclesiastical discipline, including: disposal
of gifts (articles 25 & 26); attendance at matins and vespers
(art. 7); preclusion of itinerant clergy (clericus vagus, 3);
excommunication (11 & 28); obligations of lectors and psalm-
ists (2 & 10); episcopal jurisdiction and privilege (23, 24,
27 & 30);monastic comportment and that of women sworn to chastity (9); a female vow of chastity (17). Pronouncements are
also made concerning: adultery (which would include article
17); murder, theft and their equivalent in gravity--swearing
before a druid (14); collusion of father and daughter to dis-
honorably obtain a bride-price (22); and the crime of believing in vampires (singular: lamia--art. 16).

Particularly important to our discussion are the prescrip-
tions concerning those clergy who would assist captives (short
of kidnapping, 32), or stand as guarantors for a pagan's debt
(but forbidden to use violence against the latter in case of
default);proscription from ministering of British clergy lacking references (33); and the prohibition of monks who wander
without abbatial permission (34). Articles 32 and 8 offer recognition that some accommodation to the non-Christian structure of Irish society was necessary for the Church's survival.
In 32 the echo of scandal-consciousness ("many clerics will be
blamed for one thief," i.e. if aid is offered to the extent of
assisting [presumably] a runaway) recalls a similar caution on
Patrick's part (Confession,48): lest others be persecuted as a
result of his having exploited (circumveni) the people among
whom he labored. Behind article 8 is the understanding that
Christians (especially in an economy based on barter) would
make contracts with non-believers. Number 33 makes stipulation
for what must have been a rather common occurrence: contacts
with wandering or settling clerics from western Britain. And
34, in restricting the movement of monks, appears, in terms of
organizational discipline (along with the other articles per-

tinent to ecclesiastical comportment) to be in conformity with the canons of the Council of Chalcedon (451).

Structurally, then, the church implicit in the First Synod is Roman in character, displaying episcopal diocesan autonomy, consciousness of its distance from non-believers, conformity for (particularly) clergy and for the laity, and a desire to regulate monastic comings and goings. As Hughes would have it, a church more evolved and organized than the Patrician church, still a minority in the midst of non-believers,and at one with Rome in its framework. That is to say, in all but one respect: marriage. As best we can observe, this document provides for a married clergy. Beginning with the Council of Elvira (c.300), and even more explicitly with Chalcedon, the universal Church did not. Surely the matter was not so easily resolved as by the passage of a series of stipulations; and, as indicated by Hughes (CEIS, 41-2), there did evolve from the 4th century on the Gaulish custom of bishops living apart from their wives after episcopal consecration.The question is not simply one of decree and conformity; there are the matters of custom and in-terpretation. Simply put: which clergy (all, or just bishops) were to be celibate? And under what circumstances? Was total separation from the marriage-partner necessary for those al-ready married? Or was it satisfactory for the couple to main-tain continence under the same roof? As is often the case in matters involving terse directive, the First Synod is more in-triguing for what it does not say than for what it does. The directive concerning a cleric's dress and his wife's obliga-tion to wear a veil (art.6) speaks of <ab hostiario usque ad sacerdotem> ("from ostiary to priest"). The word <uxor> is used to indicate "wife"--a term later Irish Latin writers felt obliged to avoid in referring to the former wife of a clergy-man (see: Bieler, Penitentials,n. 12,pp.243-4), perhaps imply-ing, therefore, that, from the standpoint of the First Synod, the orders mentioned did indeed retain a matrimonial relation-ship after ordination. We must also note that "from ostiary to priest" does not include bishop. Would this mean that bish-hops separated from their wives, but that lesser grades of the priesthood were not so required? Hughes does not offer such a distinction, and suggests (pp. 51-2) that monogamy alone would have borne enough resistance from the then polygamous Irish, without discussion of total abstinence. She concludes that the Irish Church, at this early stage (for her, the mid-6th cent-ury), insisted upon monogamy but "may have made no serious at-

34

tempt" at continence.

Perhaps the seeming ambiguity of the celibacy question reflected in the First Synod holds some degree of argument in favor of Bieler's dating (c. 457). If not, and if Hughes is correct, we cannot escape the conclusion that, for all its apparent aloofness of attitude regarding pagans, the text reveals a somewhat significant concession to, or at least recognition of, Irish pre-Christian custom.

Many measures stipulated in the text were to be justified by historical developments. About the time of Hughes' suggested dating, Gildas' writings clearly attest a strong, but not yet dominant, monastic presence in Britain (Hughes, CEIS, 43). Some fifty years later (c. 600), in his letter to Pope Gregory the Great, Columbanus informs the pontiff that Vennianus (generally accepted by scholars as the writer of the earliest surviving Irish penitential, and identified as either Finnian of Movilla or Finnian of Clonard; see: Bieler, 3) wrote Gildas on the question of monks leaving monasteries without their abbots' permission (ed. Walker, p. 8). It would appear that by Vennianus' time the movement had already begun to recognize the problem of discipline as being its own.

Indeed, the Church in Ireland as emerged in the late 6th century was unlike any Rome had anticipated. While bishops of the Roman Order and style doubtless held sway in theory, the the picture of their de facto jurisdiction is unclear and not of prime importance to Christianity Irish-style. What we do know of the evolution of the monastic church in Ireland comes largely from testimony documented generations after-the-fact. The various Irish annals are the subject of much debate as to accuracy. Hughes has pointed out the complexities and pitfalls of accepting dates and events entered before 585 A.D. (ECI, 144ff.). We recall that even (especially?) so famous a figure as Patrick evokes seemingly irresolvable contention, if not at times Byzantine argument. In fact, his very fame is for some a leading indicator of suspicion. Is the Patron's career so confusing because of annalists' manipulation of history for political ends? (If so, they made a muddle of it.) To what degree did the Saint and history create each other? Questions that appear to demand asking, and so resolutely refuse to surrender an answer. And in the midst of it all: the apparently genuine works of the man himself who so fervently bares his soul and reveals so little the 20th-century historian wants to know.

The situation is no less challenging in the case of Irish monasticism which, when first we come upon it, is already in place, apparently fully formed, and the "natural" result of mutual accommodation between Mediterranean religion and Gaelic society fused by the ardor of the desert. Accounting for the development requires cautious use of the same potentially hazardous chronicles, examination of materials descriptive of the subject--including testimony gleaned from the sometimes factual, sometimes fabulous, always intriguing hagiographic data, the Lives of the Saints.

The most succinct outline of monastic evolution presents itself as the so-called "Catalogue of the Saints of Ireland" (Haddan and Stubbs, II ii, 292f.--also termed: <De tribus ordinibus sanctorum Hiberniae>, Heist, 81-3). Three neat stages of development are shown being the periods (dated by Hughes, CEIS,70): 1) the "holiest," beginning in 432 with Patrick, extending through the reign of Tuathal Maelgarb (obit.: AU 548; CS 544) and characterized by episcopal order, one tonsure, one mass, one Easter, and the company of women not being rejected; 2)the "very holy," from the reign of Tuathal's successor Diarmait mac Cerbaill through that of Aed mac Ainmere (obit.: AU 597; CS 598) and composed of few bishops, many priests, different rites, many rules, one Easter, one tonsure (albeit the last two are "irregular") and women are avoided and excluded from monasteries; the ritual of the mass is accepted from the "holymen of Britain," David, Gildas and Docus; it is the age of Finnian, Enda, Ciaran, Columba, Brendan, Kevin and Lasrian (among others); 3) the "holy," lasting after the 2nd order until the great plague (AU 664) and characterized by a majority of priests inhabiting desert places, condemning the ways of the world, and having diverse rules, various rituals, tonsures and celebrations of Easter. The contentious nature and bias of this document have been discussed: Grosjean clearly demonstrating that it was composed (9th or 10th century?) at a time much later than the Third Order it claims to be contemporary with. Nora Chadwick (Age of the Saints, 71ff.) has underlined the fictitious nature of the text wherein the succession of the Three Orders is presented so as to create the impression that monasticism (in particular its anchoritic feature) was an inferior symptom of evolution from a time of greater Roman "sanctity" and stability. As Chadwick states: "the so-called Third Order has always been an integral part of the monastic church."

The complexities of debate implicit in this document are beyond the chronological scope of this study. It should be noted, however, that whatever falsehoods may be present in the "Catalogue," the tradition of British Saints playing a role in the Irish Church was strong and persistent enough to be deemed evidence sufficiently plausible to be used in church debate long after the age of the monastic founders had passed. And we cannot fail to note the inclusion in the same Order of both Gildas and Finnian--the latter quite possibly the same Vennianus (latine) referred to by Columban as having had correspondence with the former on the matter of monastic discipline.

Monasticism did not,therefore, "grow out of" the church implanted by Patrick and any other partially forgotten missionaries. It did, rather, grow with it and within Irish society until the old and the new produced a symbiotic basis for continuity instead of conflict. To be sure, there were points of contention, as we shall see; but not of a type to submerge the native culture and stifle its genius.

It must be understood as clearly as possible: Ireland was the first European country to accept the religion of Rome by means other than the wake of Roman conquest. Unlike their kindred in Gaul and much of Britain, the Irish never suffered the wholesale dismantling of their institutions and customs so as to make way for the rule of legions and the administration of Caesar to be followed eventually by the diocesan (a military term) structure of the Church. Unlike Calgacus, they had no need to say of Romans, "Where they lay waste,they call peace." At the moment of Patrick's coming, as for generations thereafter, Ireland's society was composed of a myriad of small warlord realms (called tuatha, "peoples") each jealously guarded by a fighting elite whose chieftain claimed the title of king (ri) and based his nobility and claim-to-fame on exploits-in-arms, as well as the number of "clients" (celi) in his dependency (Mac Niocaill, 60). The latter concept was founded on mutual obligation between lord and man, involving exchange of "rented" land and animals for yield and services.The degree of flexibility and protection for both parties varied according to the nature of clientship:either free (which was terminable) or base (which was not). The nobility and all members of society had their "worth" carefully determined in terms of specific measure: toward the end of the 7th century, for example, a petty king (the lowest level being called ri na tuath--literally, "king of the people") had an honor-price of approxi-

mately 49 milch cows (Mac Niocaill, 42). Such "value" was tak-
en into account in cases of harm for retribution, or when testimony was to be given--the higher the rank, the greater the
weight of word. And the higher the potential forfeit.

So much is understandable in practical terms. Old Irish
society was more than just hierarchical in economy. There were
what we might call spiritual obligations as well. From top to
bottom each individual was conceived as fulfilling a function
necessary to the harmonious survival of the whole. At the top,
the king: in theory married to the tuath, therefore father of
his people. His well-being, perfect physical state and proper
comportment were vital not only for success in battle, but for
preserving the balance of the group's existence. Without that
harmony, ill could befall society: crop failure,stillborn cattle, plagues, any sort of what modern man would term "natural
disaster." But for these people "natural" did not mean the
result of climatic, biological, or ecological happenstance; it
implied the predictably horrendous result of the disruption of
order, perhaps in the king's case because of the violation of
some taboo or failure to comply with obligation. In either the
positive or negative sense, this idea of duty was covered by
the term <geis>. And the king's proper role, ideally at least,
was conditioned by a myriad of geasa (plural),involving dress,
etiquette, habitation, protocol, honor, generosity--all phases
of his existence. If the king were good, one could tell by the
prosperity of his people; if bad, the opposite would obtain.

Beside the king would be his druid, functioning not only as
"holyman" and advisor,but as repository of knowledge and guar-
dian of a tradition both ancient and oral which included aug-
ury, magic and a compendium of lore. Throughout Irish history
and from time immemorial the druidic "order" had undergone evolution and change, so that its members included those of various stages or grades and functions: interpretors of the "law"
(which was based on custom), keepers of the memory of the people's past, genealogists, seers, poets--practitioners of all
types of wisdom. Their education was long, arduous and unending. Their class was not the same at all times and places among the Celtic peoples. Among the Gauls, according to Caesar
(Gallic Wars, Bk. VI), the druids exercised a power of life
and death such as not observed in Irish tradition where they
are depicted as advisors and men of wisdom,but definitely sub-
servient to the king.

Beneath the king in rank were the nobles who, as he, claim-

ed wealth and prestige from clientship and prowess-in-arms.
Since in the strictest sense kingship was not hereditary in
Old Irish society--all male descendants of a previous king being eligible until the fourth generation to hold the kingship
(Mac Niocaill,54)--it behooved the nobility to be conscious of
its pedigree and the possibility of qualified members rising
in status to the head of a tuath or higher, perhaps as over-
lord of a group of peoples.

Lowest in rank among those of status was the free peasant-
ry: the workers, the producers of society. Of these the highest in grade was the <bo-aire> ("cattle husbandman"), defined
as a self-sufficient farmer (Mac Niocaill, 65), most likely of
commoners to be able to change his status upward by judicious
ous application of clientship.

There existed also a sort of in-between class of craftsmen
called <aes dana> whose skills varied from poet to wright. The
more skills one had the higher he could move from commoner to
noble rank, for knowledge of any special kind was considered
something close to a divine gift.

The classes briefly outlined above constituted that part of
Old Irish society which was free and, thereby, had rights, including full participation in functions, feasts and rituals,as
well as protection prescribed by custom and law, and a place
among kin. Less fortunate were servile groups composed of native Irish, unransomed prisoners of war,and slaves captured and
sold into Irish society. Although technically without rights,
they could not, like chattel,be assigned in clientship as part
of a fief (Mac Niocaill,68). In theory it was possible to rise
from this lowest of circumstances; in fact, short of good fortune and talents, odds must have been very much against it.

This latter was a problem confronting Patrick from the be-
ginning--who would have been better prepared to oppose it? We
recall that parts of his defence and letter refer to his converts who are enslaved (for example, Confession,42;Letter,14).
From what he tells us and from the 7th article of the First
Synod, that unfortunate condition did not preclude entry into
orders in the Church. By the time of the Church's integration
into the Irish legal system (7th-8th centuries), however, the
granting of noble status to the clergy would seem to have made
it impossible for someone still in servitude to become ordain-
ed.This does not imply in the least a slackening of Church opposition to the practice. It merely underscores acceptance of
prestigious (and, therefore,effective) rank in compliance with

native tradition.Let us not forget that slavery--including far worse forms of it--would persist into the 19th century (and even later) in most parts of the world.

Even this superficial description should enable us to appreciate the extraordinary problems facing Patrick in his mission.We can readily intuit the continuing pitfalls confronting his Roman-oriented successors who had none of the "civilized," urbanized, tamed material of dead empire to work with.   What they did have was an integral,unconquered people whose cultural beginnings were beyond memory,whose values were at least to some degree still those of the continental Indo-European Heroic Age, and whose attitudes, chiefly because of geography,were basically archaic and conservative. Given the track-record of Rome's other conversions, it would have been strange had the home-grown version of Irish Church structure not come to the fore.

In effect, Christianity was growing in two branches in early historic Ireland: the Roman Order with its "territorial" bishops whose dioceses would have been co-terminal with lands owned and controlled by any one,large tuath or (one could imagine) groupings of smaller tuatha;and the monastic order which for the first generation or two after the Patron's death seems to have been under episcopal command. Then what must have been an almost imperceptible erosion of episcopal governance set in.   Very few great moments in history can be chronologically pinpointed;they are usually the result of a confluence of forces. In Ireland's case, forces of native tradition, societal structure, and even the helping hand of natural disaster.

The penitential author referred to by Columban as "Vennianus" provides us with a view of monasticism as established but as yet "of no great importance in ecclesiastical administration" (Hughes, CEIS, 52). If this Vennianus was indeed Finnian of Clonard (obit. 549) and this penitential represents either his actual work or legitimate tradition, then we have solid evidence for the as yet lack of monastic dominance of Irish religious life at mid-6th century. It would also follow that Ciaran of Clonmacnois, Tigernach of Clones, Enda of Aran, and other early founders were all subject to diocesan discipline.

Governance is one thing, endowment another. Not only did the Roman idea of urban organization have to make major structural concessions in a country without towns; it had also to confront the Irish legal custom of inalienable land.   Simply

put, land was considered family property, non-disposable without the consent of all adult male members of the possessing
family.   The concept of rich individual endowment in modern
terms is,therefore,irrelevant in this context. And so,when the
heroic image of monastic challenge became popular (especially
among the upper classes which evidently offered their share of
sons to the movement), it was deemed exceedingly advantageous,
not to deed property to the Church, but (using anachronistic
terminology) to establish a trust with a monastic community
whereby the foundation would retain identity with the endowing
family,continue to operate as a religious unit of that family,
and elect,whenever available,as ruler of that community a des-
cendant of the original endowing family. Such a compromise,
supported by the influential clans of Ireland and providing
nigh-well limitless opportunities for both monastics who could
own nothing to start with and great lords who would lose nothing thereby,appeared destined to carry the day in the evangel-
izing process.   It also provided for the retention of the native integral land and family cohesive structure,while allowing
attractive flexibility for assimilating the new Faith with its
revolutionary prestigious learning and, yes, awesome power.
     After the fact, great and successful ideas often boast of a
complicity of fate. Not as often said, but at least as just-
ly put,"Fortune smiles upon the deserving." Monasticism's perhaps single mightiest aid came in horrible form. Irish annals
record for what must have been the year 549 in modern dating
the <crom conaill> or <buide conaill>,the great Yellow Plague.
Before its advent the overwhelming number of clergy recorded
were bishops; thereafter until 600 abbots outnumber bishops;
from 600 to the plague of 664 the number of abbots mentioned
is double that of bishops (Hughes,CEIS,65; MacNiocaill,102-3).
Mac Niocaill views the period "from plague to plague" (i,e.
549-666) as the "period of the great monastic foundations."
Hughes (pp.67-8) narrows the period a bit,and basing her findings on the writings of Gildas, "Vennianus" and Columban, concludes "that some great monastic <paruchiae> were being founded between about 540 and 615."   We can see from the qualifier
"some," and the broader chronology of Mac Niocaill, that these
two scholars are in fundamental agreement.
     Thus, just as the call to the desert was gaining momentum
(probably the second generation of the 6th century), natural
disaster took its toll on many leaders of the Roman organizational system. But, bishops were not the only victims of the

<buide conaill>. Ciaran of Clonmacnois, Finnian of Clonard,Tigernach of Clones and Colum of Terryglass also died in 549. How,then,can the plague be reckoned as a factor "contributing" to the expansion of monasticism? If we bear in mind the great state of flux in Irish society at the time--best illustrated by,but not exclusive to, O'Neill expansionism--and the violent picture the annals present (of apparently constant small-scale strife among ever-scrambling chieftains), it is not difficult to imagine monastic settlements as islands of stability offering refuge to the harassed facing both war and pestilence. And that is not all.For the same chieftains, who sought to advance their claims and prestige,to encourage pockets of learning and sanctuary, populated and governed by their own kindred who answered the call of the new heroism, was to solidify their interests. Later on we shall see from the career of Ireland's perhaps most influential monastic, Columba, that politics and ensuing conflict were no strangers to ascetic calling.

What, then,were these "monasteries"? The modern reader must first disabuse himself of what they were not: great, walled cloisters detached from the world. To be sure, some were tiny spots of isolated contemplation, chosen so as to be "off the beaten track,"such as still to be observed on the jagged rock-edifice of Skellig Michael, some eight miles at sea off the Kerry coast, with its still-intact beehive cells located on a man-made terrace beneath a 715-foot peak, whose enduring corbelled structure of stone has defied both centuries of merciless weather and human imagination. Or the legendary foundation of Kevin at Glendalough ("Valley of the two lakes") in Wicklow, originally intended to be a solitary place of prayer, with the saint choosing to meditate in a hilly hollow beyond the upper, least accessible lake. Or the equally intriguing site of Enda who came from Ulster all the way to Munster,there to be granted, not rich, fertile land, but the (then) barren Ara-mor,largest and last of the Aran Islands before the Atlantic, by King Oengus mac Nadfraich. Isolation did not hinder tradition from making Enda the teacher of Finnian of Clonard, Ciaran of Clonmacnois, Brendan of Clonfert and Columba. There must have been hundreds of little monastic areas which did not withstand the passing of their founders; we get but a hint of their numbers from the fact that so many of the valleys and islands in and around Ireland are famous for such settlements. (Map V)

To establish a "monastery" only two people (and not necessarily in orders) were required--a minimal community. Those which became famous--regardless of their founders' intention-- are for the most part located quite near what were important thoroughfares in ancient Ireland. Just about dead-center of the country,hard by the flow of the Shannon River (which moves roughly in a north-south direction), one of the heaviest con- centrations of important establishments (including Birr, Dur- row and Clonmacnois) offered relatively easy access to The Great Road (An tSlighe Mhor) which from prehistoric times stretched east-west clear across country from the (now) Dublin area to Galway (Dudley Edwards, 191; Hughes & Hamlin, 25). It became a traditional theme in later Lives of the Saints to de- pict some of them as seeking peace from the world; but surely many of the places which gave rise to thriving institutions must have been occupied, on the contrary, for their accessi- bility. And such is only to be expected,once we understand the purposes of monasteries.

If, as has often been (falsely) promoted to be the case, the great founders simply wanted "to get away from it all," it is doubtful that the movement would have had the impact it did on Irish society. It has already been implied that there was more to the matter than solely religious fervor (admirable as it may be in individuals) and the ascetic challenge. It would appear that bias and anachronistic thought have taken their toll, at least in some quarters, on the image of the saints. One may start by safely generalizing: most famous so- called ascetics have (even, at times, against their own will) taken quite an active role in the doings of their fellow hu- man beings. Irish monasticism is replete with examples, two of which--Columba and Colomban--will occupy our attention lat- er on. Let us remember that monasteries were established most- ly on land grants. Land means people, especially in an agri- cultural country. An agricultural country in which clientship, rent-in-kind and herds were at the economic base. Can we as- sume that, with the offering of land, the inhabitants thereof would be expelled? On the contrary. The larger institutions provided for the retention of laity (here called <manaig>) who lived separately from the regular monks and continued their normal lives as before. Except with certain advantages. The farmers' families were afforded the possibility that their children be educated in the new Latin learning, or even even- tually enter into orders. Of course, they would have to con- form to Christian practices. Monogamy would be the rule at a time when the country still looked upon concubinage as normal for those who could afford it. There must also have been a structuring of life in general to the practices of the ascetics: observance of the canonical hours of prayer (varying between six and eight times in twenty-four hours, depending on the institution) might require some lay assistance; scheduling according to the liturgical calendar, with special attention and celebration on feast days (including that of the founder, once he had passed on). All in all, therefore, the monasteries must have presented a great deal of stability with their usual protection by the great families who must have regularly "made the rounds," as per the custom of chieftains in their holdings.

Then too, these were places of hospitality and refuge for those seeking them. We have seen the importance of custom in old Irish society. Part of that custom required hospitality that was sacred in nature--a necessity in a country where communal and family responsibility were key to the fabric of that society. Succinctly put: an absolute (if at first unwritten) law that succor be offered to needy travellers and strangers at a time when lodgings might otherwise have been beneath the nearest tree. Once a person was taken under his roof, then, it was the host's duty to protect him at all costs. Closely related to this idea was the principle of sanctuary: custom provided sacred meeting areas for feasts, negotiations and arbitration, as well as places marking objects of pre-Christian veneration--wells, springs, trees, burial spots and the like. All off-limits to violence and pursuit. Such being mandatory in pagan tradition, the Church could do no less.

An interesting part of the Life of Ruadan (obit.584),founder of Lorrha, deals with just this question. A certain Aed Guaire killed a king's man and was offered protection by Ruadan. Diarmait mac Cerbaill, the king, nonetheless, seized the fugitive and brought him back to Tara. Ruadan and his people marched to Tara to confront Diarmait, with the result that king and holyman engaged in a cursing contest.Eventually Diarmait,who had had a frightening dream the previous night relented, but not before uttering: "Thy place shall be empty, and pigs, its inhabitants, shall root it with their snouts." To which Ruadan retorted: "Many hundreds of years before that shall Tara be empty and without any inhabitant unto eternity." (See: Codex Salmanticensis, ed. Heist, p.165.) Ruadan did get to reclaim Aed Guaire,but to his curse was attributed the doom

which came upon Tara. Historically speaking, we know that Tara
was used as a royal residence for at least another century--
perhaps until the plague of 664 (Kenney, 392). The point is
not literal fact, but the sanctity of sanctuary and the image
of the saint, not as one given to meek and gentle piety,but as
both inheritor of druidic magic and representative of the new
religion--continuator of the old within the new.

Fosterage was another feature which the Irish Church adopted from old Irish society. It was an ancient and prestigious
institution whereby children of those who could afford to do
so were raised and educated apart from their parents. The hon-
or so attached is poetically illustrated in the Compert Con-
Culainn ("The Birth of Cuchulainn"), wherein the nobles of
King Conchobor's entourage vie to rear the newly-born hero.
In the end it is judged fitting that each should contribute
his or her best skills to Cuchulainn's upbringing. A favor-
able presage of greatness to come. The sufficiently large
monasteries continued this practice with Christian adaptation
(Hughes & Hamlin, 9). One might safely speculate that this
was one of the ways by which children of Ireland's powerful
families found the call to ecclesiastical greatness, for so
strong were the ties established between foster parent and
child that Irish custom respected the relationship as being
on a par with the bonds attaching child and natural parents.

To maintain its status the monastery had to control its own
productivity. Land was set aside for cultivation of corn for
bread and gruel; vegetables were grown; wild berries and nuts
picked;apple trees were tended;pasture land reserved for live-
stock; fodder was cut for winter feed. Pigs, cows and goats
were raised--the last two also milked, providing cheese and
buttermilk; chickens and ducks supplied both meat and eggs.
Bees' honey was used as a condiment and fermented into mead,
along with beer and ale. The much cherished wine for feasts
and the sacrament was most likely imported from Gaul and the
Mediterranean. Seafood was gathered and fishing done where
available; generations later, on the Continent, Irish monastics would raise pools of great carp to provide fare. The
variety of food would seem to have afforded a balanced diet
at any time--a rather sumptuous one by medieval standards
(Hughes & Hamlin, 36ff.). Productivity also means storage,
quantities of food against winter, famine and war. Storage
means preserving: smoking, drying and salting. It means building bins. It means repair to go with mending the stone walls

between pastures, the round wooden palisades encircling the entire area, the inner concentric palisades and walls separating the clerical and lay portions of the community. It means building and rebuilding or extending quarters for inhabitants, guests and novices alike. Or constructing and maintaining a mill. As well as barns, a foundry, a blacksmith shop, stables, stiles, sties, a refectory. Not to mention a church and at least one scriptorium. Mostly all built of wood--which in turn means felling trees, curing them, splitting them, shaping them, fastening them. For the heaviest work (as for the plowing), oxen and horses; for the finest, carpenters.

In each workhouse would labor specialists: the smith shoeing horses or refitting ploughs; the cook arranging (with his mess-hands) a menu, perhaps for hundreds, including royal guests and pilgrims; the metal-worker forging tools--or his more sophisticated counterpart fashioning the details of a chalice; the scribe stretching and splitting hide to be used as parchment for a copy of a sacred or profane text, perhaps even to be illuminated in stains and inks prepared by still another specialist and bound, stitch-by-stitch, with cover adorned in semiprecious stones through the complementary art of metal-worker and monk.

Stores of food and skill meant reserves of time: to worship, to teach, to minister to the spiritual needs and physical requirements of those within and without the community. They provided the leisure to prepare the brothers for missionary work at home and abroad.

Overseeing it all was the abbot (Syriac, abba--"father"). It was usual to choose him from the family of the original land-donor. The abbot was, therefore, the <coarb> ("heir") of the original founder--especially if he was abbot of the main monastery. For there was no episcopal limit to a given monastery's <paruchia> (literally "parish"; semantically more like "province," "sphere of influence"). According to the Roman concept of organization, as we have seen, each bishop's area was bound by geographic limits. The abbatial network, on the other hand, was theoretically limitless; any monastic establishment deriving its origin by grant or alliance from a larger settlement might be considered part of that system. Hence Columba was founder of an O'Neill series of foundations which included Derry, Durrow, Kells, Iona and, technically, Lindisfarne. And it is a well-documented fact that from his time to that of his biographer Adomnan (obit. 704) only one abbot of

Iona (Suibhne, r. 652-7, whose origins are unknown) was not of the O'Neill. Abbots of those foundations looking to the mother-house for their origins were called ⟨praepositi⟩ ("those placed before") of such foundations; they too, whenever possible, were of the same kindred as their superiors.

Theologically the Irish were orthodox. Therefore, despite abbatial rule, they could not neglect the office of bishop. As the fulfillment of the priesthood episcopal rank is necessary for the ordination of priests,consecration of other bishops and (usually) confirmation of the faithful. Although honored by the Irish system, bishops did not, as such, have administrative powers. Often enough abbots were bishops as well, thus rendering the question moot. But when not, it was still the abbot who commanded his community or, if heading a main institution, a ⟨paruchia⟩. Brigit of Kildare, most famous of the women Saints of Ireland, was abbess of her own dual monastery (i.e. housing both women and men separately) and had the services of her own bishop, Conlaed. Tradition has it that not only did Brigit choose the abbot of the men's section of her institution, but that it was at her command that bishop Conlaed both baptized and consecrated bishop Tigernach of Clones.

Tradition,as reflected in the Lives of the Saints, has also ascribed many monastic "rules" to the founders of the early period. Concretely we have, perhaps, in the Regula monachorum ("Monastic Rule") of Columban (to be discussed later on) some incorporation of the "rule" by his teacher, Comgall of Bangor (Co. Down). Less tangible, however,are those attributed (among others) to Patrick, Brigit, Ailbe of Emly, Ciaran of Clonmacnoise,Brendan of Clonfert,Columba of Iona,and Kevin of Glendalough. Of these possibilities few solid traces remain. The material was reviewed comprehensively some time back by Dom Louis Gougaud (Inventaire) who concluded that the Rule of Ailbe of Emly (obit. c. 540),in Old Irish,was a compilation based on Ailbe's teachings but written by one of his successors. "Rules" of Comgall and Columba are listed (not contained) in a 9th-century catalogue of Fulda (Germany), from which Gougaud deduces that such would have been redacted into Latin--Columba's for the sake of cenobitic instruction.

It is doubtful, as McNeill states (p.81), that in the early days the founders ever circulated "rules" in written form. Surely there was no general prescription for the monastics. Each foundation must have had a set of regulations from the beginning; and as institutions expanded and flourished, espe-

ially the <paruchiae>, such would have been increasingly codi-
ied. What the traditional founders prescribed,advised,judged,
hought and commanded must have been remembered, assimilated,
ommented upon, extended by implication, later codified--in a
anner analogous to the treatment accorded the "Sayings" of
he Desert Fathers. Some of it may have been made up as one
rent along; much of it became mixed with legend or attributed
n the conventional vein--quite like the workings of hagio-
raphy. What the likes of Comgall, the Ciarans, the Brendans,
he Finnians, Ailbe, Brigit and others did and said came to
e revered, and passed on as <exempla>--"examples"--for their
ollowers. The key to understanding these "examples" has been
rell put by F.Duine (cited by Kenney, 300, n.32; translated by
he present author): "'Miracles' in hagiography are a little
ike 'examples' in preaching: it is often impossible to say
rho first put them in motion. . ." Evidently we are not deal-
ng here with literal truth, for such is the stuff of petty
inds. In the universe of prayer and veneration, in that of
ranscendent belief, the soul's poetry looks ever upward in
ope of being lifted from a world of transience and corrup-
ion to a realm that is unchanged perfection. This is not the
omputation of science; it is the experience of faith. Each
ew generation finds itself revitalized in the ever-new reve-
ations of the past; as with the Church and Scripture, text
nd tradition create each other.

As the Irish revered the memory of their saints, so also
id they retain the traditions of their pre-Christian past.
mplicit in the continuity of the founders' Rules is fidel-
ty to their own language. As the Irish Church and native
rish custom grew to accommodate each other,increasingly the
rish language appeared in clerical use (see such works as
he Martyrology of Oengus, c. 800). But not simply of an ec-
lesiastical nature. Among the oldest native-language texts
e have: the Lebor na hUidre ("Book of the Dun Cow") and the
ook of Leinster,both of twelfth-century manuscripts but pre-
senting linguistic forms deriving from at least as far back
s the 8th century, and possibly the 6th (Kinsella, ixff.).
ach text offers, along with other materials,versions of the
reat epic, the Tain bo Cualnge (the "Cattle Raid of Cooley"),
epicting the values and times of a warrior-society hundreds
f years before the advent of Christianity and recalling the
raditions of the continental Celts as classical authors describe them. A third manuscript, copied in the twelfth cen-

tury, is the first fragment of the Annals of Tigernach--composed in Latin and Irish, and containing much detail of events not to be found in the Annals of Ulster. It is to the efforts of the community at Tir-da-glas that we owe survival of the Leinster material; while the monastics at Clonmacnois copied both the Lebor na hUidre and the Tigernach (Kenney, 15). For that matter, all the so-called secular literature of Ireland enduring the ages from pre-history was copied in monastic <scriptoria> (Hughes,ECI, 165-6). This would include not merely "tales" and stories, but mythology and mythological history as well.

It may appear natural that a people, once literate, would take to recording its own past. Yes and no. Yes, because it seems to be the material to draw upon,being the most familiar. No, because such is not indicative of the record of countries Christianized to that time. Let us remember that Christianity owes its origins to a middle eastern land which had bitterly borne the burden of Roman domination and Hellenic cultural militancy in the years before the birth of Christ. It had spread to lands under the same yoke. Its missionaries, faithful and neophytes had for centuries suffered indignity, persecution and diabolically ingenious cruelty. When the Faith had emerged triumphant in the 4th century, it was to encounter internal squabbling and ever-increasing challenges ranging from administrative obligations to barbarian incursion. The 5th century was but a decade old when Rome was sacked. This to be followed shortly by a seemingly endless invasion of endless peoples. Christianity had not grown to love paganism: an innate streak of puritanism coupled with the horrors of history had seen to that. Still, paradoxically, many of the finest minds synonymous with Classical learning were leading intellectuals in the Christian community. For our purposes: Jerome, Augustine and Ambrose were all imbued with a knowledge of Cicero and Caesar, and indeed an almost identical education. Hence ambivalence arose--amusing, probably, to us in the 20th century--agonizing to them. In a famous letter to Eustochium (a Roman lady who had taken vows) Jerome describes a frightening dream in which God upon His throne had told him: "Thou art a Ciceronian, not a Christian. . ." (see: Rand,105ff.). A somewhat harsh judgment, we might think. Not for those of a time which held the Graeco-Roman past to be the root of much that was immoral. And yet, in the West history had made Latin the proud language of the Church.

What we have said concerning Ireland's never having been culturally razed by Rome's legions applies equally to her monastics' view of the pre-Christian period, particularly their own. While rejecting many single aspects of their pagan heritage--polygamy, concubinage, druidry--they retained as proud relics remote memories of epic stature and the vivid fantasy of ancient lore. There is about Irish monasticism a spirit of naive enthusiasm, almost childlike at times in its eagerness to grow, and adolescent in its desire to show what it has learned. It is the awakening from within of a people to an outside world by which it is still relatively untouched and as yet unscarred. Their experience with the past had not embittered them nor made them suspicious. Confident of their own institutions, they saw no reason to reject them; and to record was to preserve.

The Lives of the Saints give many illustrations of the continuity of Irish tradition in Christian garb--many would call it "acculturation"--perhaps better understood as the ever-present blending of past with future. It has been pointed out by many scholars that any number of monastic sites appear to have once been pre-Christian places of worship, festivals or sanctuaries (Kenney, 309ff.), or located on the boundaries of ancient kingdoms (Hughes & Hamlin, 29ff.). In fact, the two observations are complementary; it is precisely on borders of all types--in time as well as in space--that much of ancient Irish magic is evident (Rees & Rees, 94). The meeting points of provinces,farms;the conjunction of seasons;the very threshold one crosses to enter someone's home--all represent, all mark movement from one order of reality to another. Such associations have been attributed to the location of 8th-century crosses near the boundary between Kilkenny and Tipperary (P.O' Riain; Hughes & Hamlin, 29).

Monastic places apparently deriving their names from the sacred trees of pagan Ireland abound: the oak--Brigit's Kildare (Cell-dara, "Church of the Oak"), Columba's Durrow (once Dair-mag, "Oak-plain") and Derry (Daire Calgaich, "Calgach's Oak Wood"); the yew--Ailbe's Emly in Tipperary (Emly originally Imblech-Ibair, and seemingly meaning "the umbilicus of the yew," therefore denoting the primeval "center" of an ancient people's territory; see: Kenney, 314; A.T. Lucas), and perhaps the very name of Ibar ("yew") of Beggery Island (Kenney, 311-2).

Much has been written to underscore the similarities between Brigit (whose feast day, February 1, coincides with the beginning of Irish spring and the celebration of fertility) and an identically named trinity of goddesses. She, like her pre-Christian counterparts, is patroness of learning and poetry. And as an evident continuation from prehistoric times, her nuns were reported as late as the 12th century (by the Cambro-Norman Giraldus Cambrensis) to have attended a sacred fire whose sanctuary was forbidden to men (Kenney, 357-8).

Intriguing traits suggest pagan associations with the traditions of: Ailbe of Emly who is presented as cared for by a she-wolf when he was an infant, whose father is Ol-chu ("Great Dog"), and whose very name is that of Mac Da-tho's divine dog in the boisterously comic Ulster-cycle tale of Mac Da-tho's pig (Kenney, 314); Brendan of Clonfert who has become synonymous with fantastic sea-voyage and whose adventures demonstrate continuation of the ancient <immram> (voyage tale) transformed by Christian content and redirected by monastic overseas travels (Dillon & Chadwick,196 and 265); and Senan of Scattery Island who, perhaps like Ibar, Ailbe and Brigit, owes his name to some pagan deity--in this case that of a sea-god who controlled the waters of the Shannon's estuary (Kenney, 364).

Characteristics like the above among the Irish saints give the impression of being endless. How many traits recalling the pagan past were literally true or to what degree is often impossible to ascertain. By what measure do we judge a "degree" of paganism, or "truth," for that matter? Is it "pagan" for a monk like Ruadan to curse Tara? Did not Christ say of Judas that it would have been better had he never been born? Is it "magic" to struggle with evil spirits? Did not Christ cast out devils? And, if invoking God's Name may bring good, why, for justice's sake, is it wrong to bring down His wrath as well? Concerning matters so monstrous as the Viking practice (called <gallcherd>--"foreign art") mentioned in the Life of Cainnech, whereby children were thrown on spears for amusement, we may flatter ourselves by implicitly consigning them to another age by means of the epithet "pagan." But there are distinctions to make which command control more exacting than cultural finicality. First we might recall that not all the Irish people were converted at the same time and with the same thoroughness. Next we must realize what the nature of our evidence is. The larger portion of it comes in its present form from a time centuries after the alleged facts described. This is not to deny the possibility of historical events being re-

51

flected in what we have; but, as in the case of the Lives, we are compelled to be aware not only of the time-factor involved, but of the perspective of the copyist(s), the accretion of lore ("pagan" and otherwise), and the many recensions and variations reflecting alterations to accommodate changing tastes, customs and values. Sometimes one age would simply have forgotten or been shocked by the "ordinary" doings of another; or old alliances and claims had to be "adjusted" to new experiences and realities.

We should try to distinguish between what we might be tempted to call "pagan" and what is quite simply a survival that in religious terms is neutral, but culturally significant. For example, a saint's genealogy. This was of prime importance in a land of clans (thatha) and fierce rivalry. Brendan is of the Ciarraige; Declan of the Deisi; Ciaran of Saigir of the Osraige on his father's side, but of the Corcu Loegde (who claimed to be the first people Christianized in Ireland) on his mother's. Many, if not most, of the saints are of noble birth. Such notice established the individual's pedigree, the honor of his people, the unique blessing brought to his kindred and associates, and the legitimacy of claim made by his venerable foundations. Surely this is not limited to "pagan" practice. Nonetheless it is a metamorphosed continuation of pre-Christian genealogical consciousness.

Plummer (VSH, cxxixff.) made an exhaustive study of what he called "Heathen Folk-Lore and Mythology in the Lives of the Celtic Saints." He concluded that there was a great deal of both in the material. To the contrary, Kenney (p. 302) correctly suggested that, apart from the cases of Brigit and a few others, the Lives demonstrate the retention of much magical lore, but little mythology as such: the saints are not portrayed as divinities; they were, however, "the heroes of the new order." What we have, then, in Kenney's term, is an amalgam of "magic" and "superstition" blended with Christianity. As we might say, a retention of the old in the new. What the Lives and much of the rest of the information about the early Irish saints tell us--as we keep the reservations imposed by chronology and culture--is how they were viewed through time and by the people for whom they served as examples and who, in turn, served their legends. As inheritors of an ancient lore and way of life, they were to assume by degrees and stages a significant part of the order of the past. As the new holymen possessed of the new power, they

were increasingly looked upon as guardians of heritage and
spiritual harmony; we dare say even as the "new druids." We
need not be surprised, or consider it an abasement of Christianity: it was the same 6th century which produced the illustrious Gregory of Tours, scholar, statesman and defender
of orthodoxy, who, when in ill health, would regularly drink
as an elixir, some water mingled with dust from inside the
coffin of a saint (Book II of Miracles, chap. I).

Like their ancestors, inspired by the urge reflected in
the <immrama>, the "heroes of the new order" did not choose to
limit their mission to their homeland. They found another
challenge: exile for Christ in service beyond the sea. Just
as the men of Ulster struggled to implant Gaelic culture on
the western shores of Britain, and as Christian influence had
rippled to Ireland from Gaul, so now would the tide return
bearing Columba to Argyll and Columban to the Continent.

V   THE TWO DOVES

From ages immemorial the Irish had been fascinated by the
challenge of the sea. Before the Christian era a whole tradition had developed around the search for the Otherworld,
the abode of immortal gods and heroes, often referred to as
the Land of Promise (Tir tairngiri) which was perhaps to be
found beyond the horizon in some distant island where all is
perfection, unchanging and forever young. It was quite natural that the theme be taken up by the new Christian Order.
And so we have tales, some fictionalized (such as the Voyage of Brendan), some solidly historical (as those of Cormac
Ua Liathain; see: Adomnan, pp.440ff.; or of three monastics
who arrived at Alfred the Great's court in 891; see: D&C, 120,
135f., 143, 193f. and 265), of "Christ's soldiers" braving
the vicissitudes of tide and weather in an act of ascetic
bravery, by simply allowing the sea to take them afloat where
it would in order that God's will reveal the place of their
resurrection.

There were also other voyages undertaken as more carefully planned enterprises. The first such was Columba's. To understand it and him we shall have to consider the circumstances leading up to his decision. Most of our information on Columba derives from the Vita Columbae (Life of Columba, written
in the late 7th century by his spiritual heir and distant rel-

ative the ninth abbot of Iona, Adomnan), with additional compact references coming from sources such as Bede (a younger contemporary of Adomnan, and who does not appear to have known the latter's Life of his ancestor), the Martyrology of Angus (c. 800), two versions of a Latin Life contained in both Codices Insulensis and Salmanticensis, and, in the Irish language, an apparently genuine 6th-century work the Amra Choluimb Chille (Eulogy of Columcille, allegedly composed out of gratitude for Columba's support of the <filid> by their leader, Dallan Forgaill; see: D&C, 183; Kenney, 427). While it is not always possible to distinguish between fact and pious legend, or history and literary convention, our sources do provide material sufficient to afford a relatively solid picture of the saint's career and genius.

In accordance with Irish genealogical tradition, Columba's pedigree is firmly established as one of the most illustrious of his day: he is the son of Fedelmidh and, therefore, great-grandson of Conall Gulban, son of Niall of the Nine Hostages. In brief, a scion of the Cenel Conaill, one of the great, powerful warlord families in Ireland, which held Donegal as its seat of dominion. His mother was Ethne, daughter of Mac-naue, descended of the royal house of Leinster (Andersons' edition, 186ff.). We may recall that it was he the Ui Neill who from the 5th century had embarked on a most successful enterprise of conquest resulting in seizure of large territories in northern and eastern Ireland. By the time of Columba's mature years (mid-6th century) the so-called northern Ui Neill had consolidated the areas more or less of modern counties Donegal and Tyrone, and continued to press east towards the land of the Dal Riata and south into the holdings of the Airgialla. South of the territory of the latter lay the domain of the southern Ui Neill, with its symbolically all-important control of Tara in Meath. Such is an over-simplification of the respective hegemonies, but can still give a general idea of the dynamics of influence in what was to say the least a very fluid and not always clear situation--subject to change and revision from battle to battle and from negotiation to negotiation. Key to the political issue was the kingship of Tara with its mighty prestige and geographical advantages of centrality and fertile land. It is the opinion of scholars like Nora Chadwick (D&C, 181ff.) that the so-called high-kingship of Ireland (centered at Tara) was a relatively late fiction of the Ui Neill in order to gain legitimate control of as much of the area as possible. This, in addition to the seizure of the ancient Ulaid capital, Emain Macha, a scant two miles from Armagh and its tradition of Latin learning, would create a neat package of political, cultural and religious claim for the holder.

Into such a climate of ambition was Columba born. But he was not to be a warlord like so many of his kin. According to Adomnan (and what is so often seen as a commonplace in the Lives of the Saints), Columba's mother, even while her son was still in the womb, had a dream wherein an angel predicted her son's sanctity. Actual experience or not, Columba was fostered (in accordance with Irish custom) while still a child to a priest named Cruithnechan, and early on began his religious training under a bishop named Findbar (also known as Vinniavus). Just who the latter was is a point of contention (see: Andersons, pp. 68ff.). The two likely possibilities are Finnian of Movilla (known to have been a bishop, and whom later tradition in the Lives places in conflict with Columba over the latter's unauthorized copying of a biblical text) and Finnian of Clonard (whom tradition associates with many saints as their teacher). It would most probably be while studying with whichever of these men that Columba took this name so as to signal his entry into orders as a deacon. For, according to the Martyrology of Angus, his given name had been Crimthann; now it became Columba. Thus the "fox" (Crimthann) of this world gave way to the Church's (-cille) "dove" (Colum). Thereafter, we are told by Adomnan, he went to the land of the Lagin (i.e. Leinster) to study "divine wisdom" under an ancient master named Gemman (Andersons, 382ff.). But, rather than elaborate upon Columba's educational experience, Adomnan mentions it incidentally as framework for illustration of the saint's terrible powers (and as what we may consider an example of the awe in which the Irish held their holymen). One day, when Columba was a short distance away from his master who was reading, a young girl, attempting to flee an attacker (described as a persecutor of innocents), ran up to Gemman who called Columba for help. Disregarding the monks, the attacker speared the girl right under their robes; she fell dead upon their feet (super pedes eorum) as the killer moved off. Gemman cried out for vengeance. So Columba cursed the murderer, prophesying that in the very hour the victim's soul would rise to heaven, her attacker's should plunge into Hell. The murderer dropped dead. Mere example or literal fact, this

would not be the last instance of Columba's championing the
defenceless. Adomnan (II, 33) reports Columba warning Broichan (druid of Bruide mac Maelchan, king of the Picts) that
death would overcome him presently if he did not release an
Irish woman he held slave. Only after falling dangerously ill
did Broichan comply.

Settings somewhat more credible involve two of the most
significant undertakings of his career: confrontation with
Diarmait mac Cerbaill, king of Tara; and negotiations for
the settlement of a treaty between the northern Ui Neill and
the Dal Riata. To the first instance later tradition (reflected in the Codex Insulensis Life of Columba and the Codex Kilkenniensis Life of Lasrian) has added details not always admitting a distinction between fact and pious fantasy.
What we have as presented by the Annals of Ulster (A.D. 560,
recte 561) and Tigernach is the battle of Cuil Dremne won by
the forces of the northern Ui Neill in alliance with those
of the king of Connacht over Diarmait mac Cerbaill. An entry
in Tigernach for the previous year lists the death of Curnan,
son of the king of Connacht, while under the protection of
Columba, at the hands of Diarmait, as one of the causes of
the battle. Fascinatingly enough, credit for the victory is
attributed to the saint's prayer wherein he refers to the
Son of God as <mo drai> ("my druid"). Both Adomnan (writing
sometime shortly before 700) and the much later Insulensis
Life mention a synod at Tailtiu (Teltown, Meath) whereat, probably in 562 (see: Andersons, 73-4), a sentence of excommunication was passed upon Columba, for reasons Adomnan labels
"trivial" (veniabilibus, III, 3) without specifying what they
were and which the later Life of Columba attributes to his
having made an unauthorized copy of a Gospel and Psalter manuscript brought from Rome by Finnian of Movilla--a copy Diarmait mac Cerbaill ordered Columba to surrender to Finnian.
Since Columba is cited by the Annals as going to Iona in what
scholars accept as 563, and Adomnan stresses that the voyage
took place in the second year after the battle of Cuil Dremne,
legend has interpreted the move as a pious undertaking in ex-
piation for the guilt associated with such bloodshed. Consequently the Life of Lasrian depicts Columba accepting the order of his <anmchara> (confessor and soulmate) to go into permanent exile (ed. Plummer, II, 139); and the subsequent founding
of the island monastery has been seen as part of that self-im-
posed penance.

Actually nothing of the sort seems to have been the truth. Whatever "facts" may obtain in the career of Columba--whether certain incidents ascribed to him took place or are fictionalized accretions illustrative of historical conditions or issues--it is certain that he was deeply involved in the politics of his day. This should not be surprising or seem improper. For reasons observed, Ireland was a place of great struggles and dynamism in the 6th century, despite or even because of dynastic conflict and occasional natural disaster. It was an age of great cultural leavening due to a relatively new religion which, with its triumphs, had to bear the responsibilities of success. If the new order was to replace the old, then the new had to prove itself capable of filling the role of the old and adding the benefit of higher calling. As both prince of the Ui Neill and monastic, Columba accepted the challenge. With his foundations in Ireland he attempted to consolidate northern Ui Neill church claims in both their home territory (Derry in 546) and in that of the rival southern branch (Durrow in, perhaps, 585; see: Andersons, 71 and 88).

Doubtless the legend of conflict over the copied manuscript and the apparently historical detail of Curnan's execution reflect deep truth concerning contemporary political interests. If we recall the conflict between Ruadan and Diarmait mac Cerbaill over sanctuary the former offered to Aed Guaire--as presented in the Life of Ruadan--and compare it to the episode involving Columba's Curnan, we sense jurisdictional controversy and a deepening assertiveness by the monks to establish Christianity as the religion of the future. If we also realize that Finnian of Movilla was bishop to the Dal nAraide (Cruithni [Picts] of modern day County Down as well as allies of the southern Ui Neill and, therefore, of Diarmait) it is difficult to resist the conclusion that the copied manuscript story is a charming metaphor dramatizing the northern and southern Ui Neill rivalry in claiming closer affinity with the new Faith.

With Columba's emigration to Iona one senses a movement toward more solidly historical attestation, due in no small measure to the testimony of Adomnan, the statements of Bede, and increasing chronicle evidence. It is Columba's successor who makes it clear that the Iona undertaking was definitely not a pilgrimage of penance, but a planned, well-organized move for which specialized companions were chosen and

authorities consulted (Andersons, 73ff.). To which might be
added, a location well-selected. First of all, had Columba
wished to find a place of isolated mortification, there was no
end of possibilities farther away from what was destined to
become nearly a center of traffic close to Argyll, with access to the outer islands, the endless waterways leading to
the Highlands, and to the north of Ireland. Next Adomnan suggests that before going to Iona Columba visited Conall mac
Comgaill, king of the Dal Riata, at his stronghold in Argyll.
And,according to the Annals of Tigernach (in reference to Conall's death, A.D. 573--recte 574), it was Conall who made to
the saint a grant of Iona. During his visit (Andersons, 225-
7) Columba was able to describe a battle even then under way
in Ireland which would result in a victory over the Dal nAraide for some of those--including Columba's first cousin Ainmere
mac Setne--who had triumphed at Cuil Dremne. From Adomnan's
perspective and purpose the reader is intended to appreciate
his subject's mystical power of second sight and prophecy. For
the modern historian there is, perhaps,a more tantalizing hint
as to the reasons for Columba's visit. The Andersons (pp. 74-
-5) suggest the possible identity of the battle of Ond-mone
(as named by Adomnan) with that of Moin Daire-Lothair (found
in Tigernach and the A.U. for 562--i.e. 563). If this be correct,we see the endlessly active Cenel Conaill and Cenel nEog-
ain relentlessly pursuing a path to reduce the opposition of
the Ulaid confederation. This victory would have advanced northern Ui Neill dominion even farther to the coast and the territories of the Irish Dal Riata. (See: Map VI) In view of the
subsquent mediation by Columba, therefore,it may not be unwar-
ranted speculation to suggest that we here have evidence of
ground-work being laid for an understanding between the Dal
Riata and the northern Ui Neill.

Contrary to Adomnan's testimony, Bede (EH IV, iv) ascribes
the granting of Iona to Bruide mac Maelchan, king of the northern Picts. Mac Niocaill (p. 76) has suggested that both
statements may be reconciled by understanding Bruide as having approved the action of Conall mac Comgaill. Perhaps. We
must remark that the Annals (A.U. 559--i.e. 560) record a victory of Bruide over the Dal Riata some three years before Columba's passage to Iona. There are two possibilities. First,
that there was some resolution of boundaries by Pict and Scot
in the Argyll area before Columba's coming, allowing for the
explanation offered by Mac Niocaill. Or, more complexly, one

might see the apparent contradictions in terms of later perspective. Bede finished his Ecclesiastical History in 731; Adomnan his Life of Columba about 688/9 (Kenney, p. 432)-- certainly after 679 and before 704. Both writers see the past at a considerable distance: Adomnan almost a century; Bede still more. Bede is working in the tradition of the Angles of eastern Britain; Adomnan that of the Scots of the Hebrides and Argyll. Despite increasing contacts among English and Scots and Picts from the time of Columba to that of Bede, geography, legend and claims would tend to influence one's interpretation of what was and must have continued to be a very fluid boundary situation. In view of Columba's career of negotiations subsequent to his arrival in Argyll, and given the apparent lapse of time between his visit to Conall (563) and that to Bruide (sometime after 575?), it would appear that Conall did hold sway over the area about Iona and to a degree sufficient for the grant made to Columba. Thereafter any understanding between saint and the king of the Picts might, as Mac Niocaill tersely proposes, have provided Bruide's "assent."

With the death of Conall mac Comgaill in 574 (A.U. 573) Aedan mac Gabrain became king of the Dal Riata, the first ordained by an abbot of Iona, and in the first such investiture in Britain. Aedan and Columba were, despite some apparent initial reservations by the latter, to remain close friends and associates as long as both lived. It was with little time wasted that in 575 Columba is seen as chief negotiator at the great gathering of Druim Cett (north Derry). Neither Adomnan nor other contemporary sources provide us with details of the proceedings. Adomnan (I, xi) does speak of Columba befriending Scandlan, a hostage of Aed mac Ainmere (king of the Cenel Conaill and son of Columba's first cousin), and prophesying Scandlan's freedom and reign over his own people. But the bulk of our knowledge derives from the Amra Choluimb Chille, quite possibly a text of 6th-century origin, re-worked in the 8th and displaying subject matter, archaic word-forms and the <berla na filid> ("language of the <filid>") characteristic of the poets of Ireland. From the prefaces to the various manuscripts (see: Kenney, 426-7) we gather that Columba succeeded in three aims at the convention: freeing Scandlan, prince of the Osraige, as hostage to Aed mac Ainmere; establishing peace between the men of Ireland and the Irish in northern Britain; defence of the satirists (filid) of Ireland. It is in connection with the last accomplishment that the work is

59

alleged to have been composed in praise (amra--"eulogy") of Columba by his contemporary Dallan Forgaill, chief of the <filid>.

From the above it is possible to postulate Columba's aims at Druim Cett. But first we must consider the power politics of his age. Dal Riata, Dal Fiatach and Dal nAraide were formed into a coalition of Uladia, with Dal Fiatach usually retaining overlordship of the group. The king of Uladia at the time of Aedan mac Gabrain's accession was Baetan mac Cairell who thereupon established his authority over Dal Riata by having Aedan render hostages. This meant that Dal Riata, with its territory split between Ireland and Scotland had to pledge a levy of men in time of war as well as the support of what must have been a fleet considerable enough to secure its claims to a good deal of irregular coastline territory. It would also insure a counter-pressure on the Ui Neill should ever-possible conflict arise. At Druim Cett an alliance between Dal Riata and the Ui Neill (represented by Aed mac Ainmere) relieved Dal Riata of such obligation to Dal Fiatach, assured Dal Riata of a powerful friend to the west of Dal Fiatach, and freed the Scottish Dal Riata to maintain its forces when needed for its primary objective--defence of its own domain. The Ui Neill in turn gained what Dal Fiatach lost: an ally at the north-eastern limit of Ireland and coastal security provided by Aedan's ships. (See: Mac Niocaill, 77-9.) We know that Aedan was given greater freedom of enterprise, for it is in the early 580's that he was able to make efforts against both the Orkneys and the Isle of Man, and later on, to his undoing, to move against the Angles of north-east England. A preface to the Amra Choluimb Chille neatly sums up the concluding principle resolved at Druim Cett: "...the levying and hosting go with the men of Ireland. . .hosting always goes with the land; tax and tribute with the men of Britain," (see: Andersons, p. 40). That is, distinction was made between the two parts of Dal Riata: those in Ireland were obliged to render military aid, those in Britain payment in whatever kind. In effect, so long as the treaty was honored and the bonds between the descendants of Neill and Riata held, the latter were largely free to pursue their own interests.

As to protection of the <filid>, what has been suggested concerning both the Irish attitude toward their native culture and the role of religion in an archaic society applies.

Ireland's greatest native saint, by his efforts at Druim Cett,
not only established the means of conciliation between the old
beliefs and the new, not only opened the door to sharing the
new methods of recording and preserving ancient lore, but also
put his people uniquely on record that the purchase of man's
salvation does not require the price of jettisoning his sacred past. The druidic order was fading away; its priestly days
were numbered; but in the <filid> its memory, its values,codes
and heritage--Ireland's heritage--would survive.

Columba also moved to secure Dal Riata's foothold in Britain. As an experienced arbitrator, scion of a powerful war-
rior-family and representative of a new and expanding religion, he approached the king of the Picts, Bruide mac Maelchan, in his own keep at Inverness. The undertaking does raise
serious questions for us. As we have observed, Bede claims
that Iona was granted by Bruide (or at least his permission
for occupation was given), and this out of gratitude to Columba and the Irish monks who had converted the Picts. This may
seem to imply that Columba had visited Inverness long before
the events we have just described. It is just possible that
he did visit Bruide before Druim Cett. Whatever the sequence
of events, tradition reflected in Adomnan's work attests that
Columba did secure some sort of understanding from the king
of the Picts during his stay with him. Unfortunately for
later historians, Adomnan's purposes were not their purposes,
but mainly to recount the miraculous attributes of Iona's
founder. We are informed, however, (II, 42) that Columba
did arrange an agreement of safety for Cormac Ua Liathain,
who was engaged in monastic <immrama>, should Cormac land in
the Orkneys. Perhaps this is pious tradition's way of mask-
ing and transmuting an understanding between Bruide and Dal
Riata concerning subsequent expeditions by Aedan mac Gabrain
who could hardly have moved against the Orkneys and the Isle
of Man without the assent of his Pictish ally.

A look at a map (see: VI) of western Scotland and the north
of Ireland helps us understand Columba's intentions in choosing Iona and playing a major role in contemporary politics.
Aside from the strategic military advantages to both the Ui
Neill and Dal Riata from Columba's activities, there is also
that of cultural and religious prestige: the move to Iona
shifted for the time being the center of gravity of church
power to an independent location which, in turn, made possible
a budding union of Pict and overseas Scot eventually to result

in the formation of the Kingdom of Scotland in the 9th century. From Iona access to the Hebrides and the mainland colonies of Scots is obvious; as it is to Ireland and the Uí Néill dominions. The endless rivers and lakes of northwest Britain afforded, in a time of small-craft travel,relatively easy communications with: Britons of the Clydeside; Picts beyond the mountain "Spine" of the Highlands and Inverness; and, moving across the Clyde-Forth isthmus, even with the Angles of Northumbria. A veritable network for conversion, cohesion and the dissemination of culture with as its focal-point the tiny island off the lower peninsula of Mull.

In Adomnan's demonstration of Columba's sanctity, as well as in legends attributed to him, one note rings most clearly: his resourceful use of the world's materials to build according to the specifications of a higher vision above the conflict of tribal violence and paganism. Columba came from a fighting tradition to affect not conflict but a new harmony: insisting that Finnian of Movilla's manuscript was to be copied and shared by all; forging friendships with Pict (Comgall of Bangor, who was at Druim Cett and who later traditions claim accompanied Columba to Inverness; or Bruide mac Maelchan), Scot (Aedan mac Gabrain), or a man of Munster (Brendan moccu Alti of Clonfert); championing slave-girl or royal hostage (Scandlan); investing the energies of an invigorated Gaelic society to spread its advantages of culture, technology and humanitarianism.

There is a mythic element to the image of Columba which has come down to us, more than just that of an energetic miracle-worker whose fame Adomnan sought to perpetuate. More even than the great magician who with prayer chases the monster of Loch Ness (Vita Columbae, II, 27). It is the Columba of his final moments (III, 23) whose death is foreseen by his faithful milk-horse as it lets its tears fall upon its master's lap. The saint ascribes the creature's knowledge to a revelation by God, a type of understanding beyond the ken of rational men. We are reminded of the special communion holymen traditionally enjoy with the dumb beasts of the earth; for such saints have retained or regained their primal innocence. But there is more. Perhaps due to the ninth abbot of Iona's (conscious or unconscious) recollection of native Irish heritage ultimately derived from common Indo-European stock: for the Greeks, it was Achilles' swift Xanthus who predicted his master's death; for the Gaels, the

mute, but more touching Gray of Macha whose tears of bloo
drop on Cuchulainn's feet. In Columba the hero has exchang
ed his halo of rage for a crown of gentler light; the warrio
of death has become Christ's soldier of life.

Columba's move to Iona set in motion a new fashion fo
Irish monastics: overseas missionary work. It must be noted
however, that the term "missionary" might be misleading. "Pil
grim" (a corruption of the Latin <peregrinus>) is more ac
curate, for quite often work among non-believers or even nom
inal Christians appears to be incidental to their exile fo
Christ. That is to say that these inspired transients wen
abroad mostly for the sake of going, undertaking to leave
beloved homeland as an ascetic exercise in pursuit of salva
tion, imposing on themselves the absence of loved ones an
familiar surroundings that they might earn admission to th
homeland (patria) of the blessed. Wandering of this type ha
been explained in several ways--we have alluded to the paga
Irish practice of <immrama>, itself a source of literary in
spiration both religious and secular--it was, whatever th
sum of contributing factors, not a journey to and return fro
a particular geographic spot (as "pilgrimage" is commonl
understood to mean), but a self-abandoning, open-ended searc
for the "place of resurrection" to be revealed by God to th
individual. Strictly speaking, therefore, Columba's move wa
not an example of such;it was, instead, another "dove"--Colum
banus--who more accurately cast the mold.

What we know of him derives mainly from the following:
brief reference as related by Bede (EH, II, iv) in citing th
text of a letter by Lawrence, Archbishop of Canterbury, to th
leaders of the Irish Church (604-5); a Life of Columban (Vit
Columbani) published in 643 by Jonas (a monk who had come t
Bobbio shortly after its founder's demise); an encapsulate
version of some of Jonas' information contained in the mid
7th-century Gaulish chronicle known as "Fredegarius" (IV, 36)
two Lives of Saint Gall (apostle of Columban) by the 9th-cent
ury authors Wettinus and Walafrid Strabo; and,most concretely
a significant body of writings by the saint himself,including
six letters,thirteen sermons, two monastic rules, one peniten
tial, five poems, and another seven works considered "dubious
by the editor, G.S.M. Walker.

We are not sure of the pertinent dates of Columban's car
eer. That he died in 615 after being exiled from France in 61
is established by his biographer. The years of his birth an

63

oming to France must be tentatively calculated by comparative
vidence not always of the surest nature. Jonas apppears to
ave confused the names of contemporary monarchs and occasion-
lly assigned to some the wrong realms in the often divided
rankish political quagmire. Columban's second letter (to the
ynod of Gaulish bishops held in 603 in Chalons) informs us
hat he had then been among the Franks for twelve years, thus
lacing his arrival in about 591. His poem Columbanus Fidolio
ratri suo contains the line (vs.163): <Nunc ad olympiadis ter
enae venimus annos> ("Now we have come to the thrice sixth
lympiad of our years"). Which would (allowing four years for
ach olympiad) place his age between sixty-eight (four times
eventeen, just going into the eighteenth olympiad) and seven-
y-two (if having completed eighteen). If one assumes the
oem to have been written toward the end of his life (615),
hat would put his birth somewhere about 543-547. In any case,
hat would make him well over forty at the inception of his
verseas mission. (See: Walker's clear and precise summary
f the problem and evidence, pp.ix-xii.)

Columban was a Leinster man, and even before his birth his
other had a vision which anticipated his greatness--a com-
onplace so often to appear in later Lives of the Saints. We
earn that he, like Columba, was early on given a Christian
ducation; and doubtless through this formation he was cal-
ed to his future vocation. It has been suggested that Colum-
an's act of stepping over his mother after she had thrown her-
elf in his way in an attempt to block his departure from home
ay have been inspired by reading Jerome's 14th Epistle (Wal-
er, xii)--either that or Jonas' reading of the same text con-
inced him to use the image for dramatic effect. (Whatever the
ruth of the matter, the apparent borrowing is most fitting,
iven that Jerome is one of the patristic writers most fre-
uently cited by Columban.) It was then at Cleenish Island,un-
er Sinell, that he studied the Scriptures and perhaps wrote
hat commentary on the Psalter with which he is credited, but
hich is not among his extant works. If (as Walker believes,
. xviii) he did so at this time, he must indeed have been a
rodigy; for it is later on, at Comgall Bangor (Co. Down) that
e would have accepted the monastic life,sometime near the age
f twenty! That he did write a commentary on the Psalter seems
eyond doubt, for it is listed in both the St. Gall and Bobbio
atalogues of the 9th and 10th centuries respectively (Walker,
xiv). At Comgall's institution he became the most important

teacher,and remained there until the time of his pilgrimage to
France.

We can but speculate as to direct personal influence of
Columba upon Columban. Surely there must have been some contact between the two: Comgall is reported by Adomnan to have
been with Columba at Druim Cett, and the Lives of the Saints
(Plummer, II, 18) describe Comgall (who was a Pict of the Dal
nAraide) accompanying Columba on his visit to (the Pictish
king) Bruide mac Maelchan. Perhaps Comgall was there as in-
terpreter. Surely the latter's top teacher could not have
not known so influential an acquaintance of his abbot. It
must not be sheer coincidence that Columban would follow the
close and powerful influence who was his namesake.

Sometime around 590 Columban, accompanied by twelve disciples (in imitation of Christ's mission, and including the
future most famous of the group, Gall), set out for the Continent. On his way he passed through either British or Bre-
ton territory--or both (see: Jonas, i, 4-5; and Walker, xix),
as he approached his destination, the kingdom of the Franks.
To say that the region was replete with violence is an under-
statement. War, fratricide, blood-feud and intrigue seem to
have been unending from the accounts presented by Gregory of
Tours (History of the Franks, ending with the year 591) and
his continuator, the so-called Chronicle of Fredegarius. The
veritable cat's cradle of scheming and shifting of loyalties
rife among the descendants of Clovis from the time of his
death in 511 both tantalizes and confounds the mind. (See:
Margaret Deanesly, A History of Early Medieval Europe from 476
to 911,chapter xv, "The Later Merovingians," for a compact but
full disclosure.)

To appreciate what the Irish peregrini had to contend with,
some discussion of the background is pertinent. In 558 Lothar I, last surviving son of Clovis, the conqueror of Gaul,
became king of all his father's lands. Three years later,
when Lothar's ruthless career (which had included the burning
alive of his rebellious son Chramm with the latter's wife and
children) came to an end,the land of the Franks was relatively
secure to the south against the Visigoths in Septimania and
Spain, to the south-east against the Lombards in Italy, and to
the east against the more barbarous German groups beyond the
Rhine. However, aside from the warlike mentality of the individuals involved, Frankish custom, in its provision for divi-
sion of a king's territories among his sons, was then a guar-

ntee of disaster. And so it proved. Just who was right or
rong, justified or guilty in what ensued is often impossible
o ascertain, given the complexities of honor and feud,and the
rejudice of witnesses. · Basically what followed was: Chari-
ert was given what was to be the western portion of Frankish
oldings, or Neustria (named as the "new land" of conquest);
igebert received the eastern area,Austrasia ("eastern land"),
ncluding the region of the Rhine;Guntram was ceded the south-
astern zone known as Burgundy; and, lastly, Chilperic some
inor portions surrounding Soissons and Tournai (the latter in
odern Belgium). This last was a grudging concession to Chil-
eric on the part of the others who resented him as only a
alf-brother. Charibert's death in 567 occasioned still furth-
r ill-feeling resulting from consequent subdivision of his
omains.

Hatred was then particularized between the houses of Sig-
bert and Chilperic for reasons even more personal. As re-
ently landed members of a conquering warrior society the
ranks lacked not only sufficient appreciation of central
ule, but the sophistication of higher civilization as well.
hey were regarded, particularly by the Visigoths of Spain,
s barbarous and backward. The lesson of such a stigma was
ot wasted on the seed of Clovis: they welcomed and were
lattered by possible alliances with the Byzantine court of
oledo under the Arian king Athanagild. Sigebert managed to
ake to wife one of Athanagild's daughters, Brunhilda--a lady
elebrated by Gregory of Tours for her beauty, culture, and
he fact that she had embraced the Catholic Faith. Chilperic
elt himself outdone in prestige and strategy. And, despite
he presence of a ruthless and, perhaps, then underrated Fre-
egund (his mistress), he secured himself a marriage with
alswintha, Brunhilda's very sister, who also converted to
atholicism. This union soon ended in violence. Apparently
ecause of his relationship with Fredegund (whom Gregory of
ours, iv, 28, claims he had married before), Galswintha de-
anded to return to Spain. Chilperic had her strangled. As
result, countless battles and acts of reprisal would take
lace through the next generation of the two families; not
ge, nor gender, nor degree of kindred would spare them from
ach other's bloodlust.

By the time of Columban's arrival in c. 591, both Sige-
ert (575) and Chilperic (584) had been assassinated; Guntram
ould reign one more year in Burgundy; Childebert II (son of

Sigebert and Brunhilda) and Lothar II (son of Chilperic and
Fredegund) were emerging as rivals destined to clash, with
the whole of France as the prize (at Soissons in 595); and
through much of it Brunhilda (from Austrasia) and Fredegund
(from Neustria) wielded power through their children.

Religion was a still further complicating matter, and certainly not separable from Frankish politics. We must recall
that Gaul, by the last century of the Empire, had a deep tradition of Roman culture and religion: it was the land of
Athanasius in exile, Hilary of Poitiers, Honoratus, Martin,
Sulpicius Severus, Victricius and Germanus. True, it had been
conquered by Visigoth, Vandal and Lombard--all Arian heretics;
but it had seen the subsequent victory of the Franks whose
king, Clovis, married to the Burgundian princess Clothilda,
had, sometime after 493, come from paganism to the Catholic
Church. (See: Deanesly, 59f.) Thereafter Gaul was to prove
to be the country of Caesarius of Arles (bishop at the time
of the Frankish conquest of Burgundy), St. Radegunda (wife of
Lothar I, therefore mother of Guntram, Sigebert and Chilperic)
Venantius Fortunatus (a supplanted Italian who composed a
marriage-hymn for Brunhilda and Sigebert, and later fell under the saintly spell of Radegunda), and Gregory of Tours (of
old Gallo-Roman stock, witness to so much of interest to us
here). In brief, the barbarians did in some measure try to
preserve the structure of Romanized Gaul's institutions (HEME
62ff.); and one must not overestimate statements as to the
level of barbarism under the Frankish kings (Walker, xxii).
Neither must one underestimate it. By the late 6th century
the Code of Justinian had fallen from use, groundwork was being laid for alliance between Papacy and Frank; and there remained a presence of Latin clergy. However, regardless of intent, Frankish custom and law were bound to encroach upon the
Roman legal system; in church matters there was variance of
the liturgy and the calculation of Easter between Gaul and
Rome (Gregory of Tours, History, x, 23)--the Franks using the
Victorian cycle, while at Rome the Dionysian cycle had come
into effect; there were serious questions of corruption among
Gaulish church leaders; and surely the Latin tongue, spoken
fluently by men such as Gregory of Tours, had nevertheless
suffered a good degree of debasement, especially when compar-
ed with the usage of Irish monastics.

It was probably Guntram's adopted son and heir, Childebert
II, who permitted Columban and his disciples to settle their

rst community in the Vosges at Annegray. According to
nas, the work done and the relations established with the
habitants were idyllic in scene: at first the group is
ved from starvation by Columban's prayers, and the communi-
y's popularity grows with the widening recognition of the
mates' holiness. In quick order two new locations are need-
 because of the number of converts: Luxeuil and Fontaines.
t not all was destined to go well. Questions of clerical
risdiction and canonical regularity would arise. (See: Wal-
r, xxiii-xxiv; and McNeill, 159ff. for compact summaries.)
   The popularity of Columban must have been well marked by
me-grown ecclesiastics. That and what must have appeared
 unacceptable comportment on his part and that of his com-
nity could only have excited their jealousy and incited
eir wrath. The clearest statement forbidding clergy to
inister outside their churches and commanding monks in par-
icular to accept episcopal discipline had been produced at
alcedon in 451. Frankish clerical decrees of the 6th cen-
ury had unequivocally reinforced this and had insisted on
piscopal consent for the establishment of a monastery; in
ffect proscribing many of the autonomous facets so familiar
o Irish monasticism. And then, there was the Easter question
-so grave an issue and so persistent a theme hereafter in the
bjections of writers like Bede in criticizing the Celtic
hurch. To a mind of modern values this matter may seem out-
f-sorts with what appear to be points of larger import. One
ust realize that in an age of greater spiritual immanence
han ours it was of the highest significance that the feast
roclaiming the eternal reclamation of mankind--and a feast
ot so much remembered as relived--required computation of the
reatest accuracy and care so that its measure might be syn-
hronized with that universal structure known as creation,
ashioned and symmetrized by the divine and benevolent Hand.
ence an almost obsessive search for the perfect Paschal cy-
le. Simply put, the task was to find the number of success-
ve dates of Easter after which, and always, the dates would
epeat themselves. A somewhat naive object of research, based
n the assumption of celestial symmetry. Unfortunately man's
alculations are not God's: the vernal equinox is not con-
tant in its dating, nor, therefore, can computation based on
 fixed dating thereof be valid. In any event,Rome had modifi-
d its method of calculation through the centuries. The Irish,
ecipients of a method (which assumed March 25 as the equinox

and was based on a cycle of 84 years) outmoded at Rome fro
343, were at odds with both the Roman Dionysian system (havin
a cycle of 19 years and March 21 as the equinox) and that o
the Franks (with its Victorian cycle of 532 years and March 2
as the equinox). As if this were not enough for confusion, th
Irish celebrated Easter on that Sunday falling from 14 to 2
days after the first full moon after the vernal equinox; th
Romans from 15 to 21 days; the Franks from 16 to 22 days.

It is in relation to these difficulties,especially the Pas
chal controversy, that Columban wrote the first of his extan
epistles, addressing it in 600 to none other than Gregory th
Great. The letter is extraordinary for its precious style (th
salutation alone is thirty-three words long), its freedom o
expression,and its excellent use of Latin idiom--cast, accord
ing to Ludwig Bieler (see his Notes in Walker, p.lxxxi) in th
rhetoric of Christian antiquity and post-Roman Gaul.   Littl
credit has been accorded Columban in terms of humor, but suc
can be perceived in his fondness for puns (bold enough to pla
on the name of Leo the Great--leo meaning "lion"--in the ex
pression: "a live dog is better than a dead lion,"   Walker
4-6), his show of erudition (revealing that his name,Columban
"son of the dove," is Bar-iona in Hebrew), and in his some
what whimsical attempt at obsequy in suggesting that his com
munication with Gregory might leave him open to a remark mad
at the sight of a scortum pictam ("painted whore), "I don'
admire the art, but I admire the nerve." The wit implicit i
such usage shows the freedom he allows himself in expressin
conviction, a familiar comfort with the Latin language, and
naive confidence in the fairness of Church authority.

Most of the letter is devoted to a defence of the Iris
computation of Easter; cited therein are supporting authori
ties: Anatolius of Laodicea (unfortunately for Columban, an
without his knowledge, a reference to a forgery) and Jerome
the idea that (according to Irish calculations) Easter ma
coincide with Passover (i.e. the 14th day after the equinox
--which led some to accuse the Irish of heresy--is dismisse
as irrelevant. He cleverly sustains his (i.e.the Irish) posi
tion, repudiates the Victorian system, and challenges Gregor
to choose between Jerome and Victorius (the method's propo
nent), with the admonition that anyone opposing Jerome's au
thority would leave himself open to a charge of heresy!

Concerning obedience to Gaulish episcopal commands, Colum
ban asks if he is to have relations with a clergy replete wit

69

e guilt of simony and adultery (i.e. contact with their own
ves); and he refers to the condemnation by Gildas of bishops
o ordain, against church canon, for payment. As to the ques-
on of monastic discipline, he requests papal guidance, and
ain mentions Gildas--this time in connection with a reply to
enquiry by "Vennianus" (most likely Finnian of Clonard) on
e matter.

Columban expresses a desire to be able to travel to Rome;
t cannot. He compliments Gregory on his book of Pastoral
le and requests a copy of his commentaries on Ezekiel. Wal-
er informs us (p.11, n. 2) that Gregory in his fifth epistle
entions having sent a copy of the former to "the priest Co-
mbus" in the year 594. From which we might speculate on
ior correspondence between the two. Perhaps Columban's act
seeking papal guidance (and support?) in the Gaulish af-
ir was not so rash as critics might think. In concluding
refers to Candidus, overseer of papal lands in Gaul, and
ves Gregory to understand that he has gotten the impression
egory would wish to answer that time has made the situation
alterable. To this Columban offers the truth--as he sees
--which is even older.

It is rather clear that Columban did not simply act with
petuosity by his appeal. He relies confidently on the equa-
imity of the pope, the weight of his own arguments, and the
rce of his tradition. He is bolstered by the knowledge that
e Frankish clergy does not enjoy an unsullied reputation;
d he has made contact on the matter with the nearest pa-
l representative. He is neither bloodied nor bowed--nor
epared to recant his position.

When, therefore, in 603 he was summoned to attend a coun-
l of bishops at Chalon-sur-Saône, he refused and forward-
d an at times reproachful (paragraph 8) open letter instead,
mmarizing his position on the Easter question, mentioning
s communication to the pope (Letter II, 5) and to Arigius,
shop of Lyon and evidently leader of the Frankish faction
posed to Columban. In essence his stated desire is for mu-
al indulgence and that he be left to his woodland retreat
w that he had lived among them for twelve years (para. 6).
parently he had no intention of submitting himself to a
aring at which the conclusions were foregone.

He was still to write a letter (3rd in Walker's edition)
metime after 604 (and Gregory's death) to a pope whose iden-
ty he did not know, therein appealing to an ancient ruling

of the Council of Constantinople that churches established
pagan lands (in barbaris gentibus, para. 3) should be govern
by their own laws. Hence implicitly rejecting Frankish eccl
siastical authority as having jurisdiction over his communit

One so popular as he was not easily disposed of. The und
ing of his welcome in Burgundian territory resulted as mu
from his own lack of judgment as from the integrity of h
character. By this time Childebert had died (595), leavi
his domains to two sons soon to be implacable enemies: The
debert (of Austrasia) and Theodoric (of Burgundy). The i
domitable Brunhilda, now a dowager queen, and with the passi
of Fredegund in 597 the greatest woman in France, enjoyed con
siderable influence over and wielded consequent power throu
the bellicose siblings. According to Jonas and Fredegariu
personal conflict between Theodoric and Columban was orches
trated by Brunhilda. Her role in the circumstances has be
disputed by scholars, some of whom deem her talented, a pr
duct of ruthless times, and much maligned. The facts are
Burgundy then faced a hostile alliance of the other parts
Gaul, plus the kingdoms of Lombardy and Spain--all becaus
of a bungled attempt to match Theodoric with one of the ple
tiful stock of Spanish princesses. (See: Walker, xxi.) Th
last thing Theodoric needed was to incur the wrath of the i
fluential holyman from Ireland. He did just that. Althoug
repudiating the benefits of legitimate wedlock, he had n
been lax in embracing a royal Frankish institution--concu
binage--and had sired no fewer than four male children. S
when, in perhaps a misbegotten try at bolstering morale b
means of soliciting Columban's support (as Walker interpret
the king's action, xvi), Theodoric (or Brunhilda) brought th
boys for his blessing, the saint responded by refusing an
predicting that they would never ascend to royal power, f
"they have come forth from brothels" (de lupinaribus emerser
unt, Fredegarius, IV, 36). Not very discreet (if an accur
ate quote), but unambiguous. From the time he was a youngste
Theodoric had admired Columban; and he was not such a fool a
to overreact. He did make an effort to conciliate with th
adamant solitary who spurned the king's gifts on one occa
sion, and afterward went so far as to predict the extermina
tion of Theodoric's line after the latter had entered th
monastic enclosure of Luxeuil with intentions of making Co
lumban adhere to Gaulish practices. Still not wishing t
transform opposition into martyrdom, Theodoric commanded Co

mban to be exiled to Besançon while a decision was pondered
to how the problem might be resolved. As things develop-
, the saint's guards showed a hands-off attitude; and even-
ally Columban made his way back to Luxeuil.

He was not to be left to himself. Brunhilda and Theodo-
c dispatched Baudulf (who had taken Columban to Besançon)
d Berthar to expel the Irishman and his monks from Gaul.
fiant as ever, Columban was finally convinced by his arres-
rs (who were loathe to use force even in so brutal an age)
at failure to comply would mean the most dire punishment
r them. The trip across country from eastern France to
e Atlantic was eventful, including: a touching encounter
Orleans with a Syrian woman whose husband's blindness was
red because of her kindness to Columban and his party;a vis-
t to the shrine of Martin at Tours;and Columban's prediction
the end of Theodoric and all his family in three years'
me. Before being put on an Ireland-bound ship at Nantes,
e also composed what we have as his fourth letter--words of
couragement to those he had left behind (Walker, 26ff.). He
ves instructions for leadership and mentions, among others,a
rgundian noble, Attala, who would one day succeed him as ab-
t of Bobbio (Jonas, II, iff.; see: Walker, p. 27 & n. 1).
s severest admonition is for unity--dissension is the great-
t danger. The saint's affectionate concern permeates each
ssage to his beloved flock. It is not without bitter-sweet
mor before his conclusion that he recalls the fate of anoth-
r Jonah (i.e. "Columba" in Hebrew), and prays that "someone
ay take the place of the whale" so he may be safely concealed
d returned to the land he desires. It was to be granted.
gain, partially due to laxness of his captors, as well as to
ntrivance of nature, he was able to elude banishment. His
ip was storm-blown back to land. And Columban walked away.

His journey across Frankish territory took him through Lo-
ar's western domain of Neustria, and eventually to the
rtheast and Theodebert's Austrasia. At Metz Columban was
aught up with by some of his Luxeuil family driven out of
rgundy by Theodoric. Walker (p. xxviii) has surmised that
ttala, future abbot of Bobbio, may have been among them. In
y event, Columban decided to leave the land of the Franks
its internecine war, and the fulfillment of his prophecy
Theodoric's extermination to the ruthless and thorough
fforts of Lothar. It would come to pass in 613.

Next the company travelled the Rhine south-east, through

what today is Swiss territory; and after Gall (one of Colu
ban's companions since he left Ireland) had risked the wra
of natives by desecrating pagan altars near Lake Zurich, th
moved into the area of modern Bregenz (in Austria) at t
eastern shore of Lake Constance. Secure and permanent se
tlement would again elude them. War's fortune came to inclu
Bregenz among Theodoric's lands. Late in 612 Columban dete
mined to continue ultimately his exile for Christ across t
Alps with the Lombards in Italy. Later tradition, attest
by Wettinus and Walafrid Strabo of the 9th century, tells
of an ill Gall who balked at finishing the journey with h
master. Accordingly, we learn, Columban forbade him to cel
brate Mass while he still lived. When later on his deathb
Columban would withdraw the prohibition.

The long and hazardous trek was almost due south, over t
Alps (Walker, p. xxix, suggests the Lukmanier Pass as the pi
grims' route), and on to King Agilulf's capital at Milan. T
later, like the majority of is subjects, was an Arian Christ
ian; but his wife Theodelinda was Catholic. This last fact
plus Agilulf's fairly recent opposition to Theodoric, ma
the royal family well disposed to the Irishman who would eve
tually be permitted to establish a community at Bobbio, whic
in subsequent generations came to house a library of man
script collections scarcely rivaled during the Middle Ages a
Renaissance.

Even now tranquility was not to be Columban's. An o
wound, concerning the so-called "Three Chapters," was des
troying the unity of the Catholic hierarchy in the north
Italy. The problem involved an edict of Justinian, issue
in 543-4, condemning works of Theodore of Mopsuestia,Theodore
of Cyrrhus and Ibas' letter to Maris on the grounds of co
taining elements which separated too definitely the two na
tures of Christ. By this act the Byzantine Emperor hope
to pacify objections of Monophysites (monos--"one"; physis-
"nature") who, vehemently to the contrary, insisted that t
attribution of more than one nature to Christ was an implic
repudiation of man's ultimate destiny which is union with Go
Most, especially exiles among heretics, would have avoided t
controversy. Columban was not most. Decidedly when Agilu
expressed interest in becoming a Catholic, but dismay ov
arguments among the faithful as to the very nature of the
Saviour. And, we might add, over a decision which Pope V
gilius in 547 had been forced to accept. This, then, was t

occasion of Columban's fifth letter, addressed to Boniface IV. Its style is flamboyant, exuberant and perhaps even impertinent. His concern is direct in its admonition: "Indeed I am saddened,I admit, by the infamy done the chair of Saint Peter" (Walker, p. 38). There is also touching naivete to his confidence and openness, to his protestations of loyalty to the Holy See, to his repeated pun on Vigilius' name (and at his expense) as he exhorts Boniface to be vigilant (vigilate, vigila), and to his favorite mention of the origin of his own name. The constant theme is the establishment and maintenance of the unity of the Faith.

The final months of his life demonstrate that desire for peace which always seemed to alternate with his instinct for controversy. He settled in Bobbio and there possibly composed some of the classical meters we have from his pen (Walker, p. 192ff.). Jonas reports that Lothar, having eliminated Theodoric's line as well as Brunhilda and now master of all the Franks, sent word seeking the good man's return. It was not to be. The exile for Christ kept his word: having ordered his staff sent to Gall in reconciliation, he died on the twenty-third day of November 615, among the foreigners he had striven to bring into the fold.

Both Walker (pp. lxviff.) and Bieler (ibid. lxxiii; and "Humanism") have evaluated his works' style, content, significance and tradition. It must be stressed that the learning and mastery of Latin at the time were considered both an accomplishment and a means to the end of learning the Scriptures. And although Columban may not be thought of as a creative writer or thinker in the modern sense, he displays both the erudition so in keeping with the tastes of his time and the facile ability to adapt his use of learned language to the task of his text. Hence Bieler detects a relative restraint of classical knowledge in addressing Gregory the Great (Letter I), a freer display of the same while communicating to Pope Boniface (Letter V), and concludes that "the artist is effectively controlled by the churchman" ("Humanism," 101). Overall his letters show a style that is direct,the disciplinary works one that is "terse," the poems a "predominantly didactic" bent, the sermons "warmer tones" ("Humanism," 100). In general, a comfortable familiarity with those authors he had read, and an erudition not gleaned from compendia or bits and pieces of grammatical illustration offered by the compilation-textbooks so popular in medieval times, but "from a study of the original works" (ibid., 99).

As to which writers were his favorites,a glance at Walker's Index of Classical and Patristic references (pp. 221-2) noted in Columban's works reveals the type of "mixed" erudition one might anticipate in a monastic author whose country received the art of writing most probably from learned refugees toward the end of the Imperial Age, and with the influx of Christianity, those most frequently cited being: Ausonius (mid-4th century Gaul), Basil (in Rufinus' translation), John Cassian,Venantius Fortunatus,Gregory the Great,Jerome, Horace, Ovid, Vennianus (probably Finnian of Clonard), and Vergil. His familiarity with Horace is perhaps most significant for the fact of Horace being virtually unknown on the Continent from the end of the Empire until the 8th century ("Humanism," 99). In the 4th Letter (to the community in Luxeuil) Bieler has detected borrowing from the historian Sallust and recollections of Vergil, Horace and Ovid; in the verses Ad Hunaldum (perhaps the name of a former pupil), Ad Sethum and Carmen Navale he composes in hexameters; in the Fidolio in Adonic meter (lines consisting each of dactyl plus either spondee or trochee) and concluded by six hexameters; whereas the Carmen de Mundi Transitu (Song on the World's Passing) might well, in its message of the ephemeral nature of things and in its medieval meter (with accent and rhyme), reflect an early stage of the author's career (Walker, lvff. & 182-97). In all, the quality of his Latin (which for the most part Walker finds "very pure"), familiarity of usage and capacity to adapt language to need witness (in Bieler's words,"Humanism," 101) "the high level of Latin studies in the early Irish monasteries."

Columban's command of Hebrew and Greek are a less easily attestable matter. And, as might be anticipated, opinions have varied greatly. Extremes of thought do have a way of driving scholarship toward the middle: just as it is difficult to accept Walker's assessment ("Use of Greek Words," p.129) that evidence for the teaching of Greek in Ireland can be supported by a passage from the very late Life of Brendan (Plummer, I, 141), or that Columban used certain Greek words because of his passionate need to express himself beyond the "sober bounds of Latin" ("Use," 127); it is also unlikely that Columban derived none of his Hellenisms directly from classical authors, or that he gives no evidence in his prose of direct knowledge of the same (Smit, 170-1). In fact, Walker's later judgment (edition, pp. lxviiff.) seems more tempered

d in accordance with available materials. Among them: ap-
earing in the Schaffhausen manuscript of Adomnan's Life of
lumba ("apparently" of the early 8th century, in Irish hand
d "probably" done in Iona--see: Andersons' edition, p. 3)
the Lord's prayer in Greek; the use of Greek expressions
Irish writings (as by Columban) so as to "enliven their
yle"; testimony from the <Amra Choluimb Chille> (ed. Stokes,
404, #123) that Columba learned Greek. From this we may
fer that some grammar, or its elements, was available to the
ish in Columban's time. Enough to teach the alphabet and
enable the literarily sensitive to gather terms from Latin
thors (classical as well as patristic) and put them to their
n uses. Later Irish generations must have had a fuller know-
edge of Greek at their disposal as evidenced by the linguis-
ic mastery of John Scottus Eriugena in the 9th century.

For Hebrew we must be even less ambitious in our assess-
nt. Here only the occasional word arises. Columban's per-
istent display of "Jonah" as the equivalent of his own name
ay serve as illustration of the fascination and delight he
akes in demonstrating so intriguing a command of this tid-
it of erudition. As with the Greek, so much more with the
ebrew.

Walker's Biblical Index presents a summary (p. 220) of Co-
umban's allusions and citations. Three-hundred and twenty-
ne by his count. Matthew is his favorite source in the New
estament (with 50 references), followed by John (26) and Luke
21); his Old Testament favorite are the Psalms (27). Oddly
nough, no use of Mark has been found. Of the total, 115 re-
erences are from the Vulgate, 51 from the preceding Old Latin
ersion, 80 are labeled "uncertain," and, intriguingly, 75 are
peculiar." Some uncertainties and peculiarities may well be
ue to faulty memory or the fate of copying. Nonetheless, if
alker's mathematics are reasonably correct (as it appears),
olumban does attest to a period of transition from one ver-
ion of the Scriptures to their revision, and , perhaps, to
he Irish having had still another variant rendering in use
efore the adoption of the Vulgate. (See: Walker, lxix.)

The thirteen sermons which are considered legitimately
olumban's are the remains of what must have been a much lar-
er body of such works. Whether or not ever committed to
riting, his homiletic output, given his energies and influ-
nce (to which Walker credits no fewer than 53 foundations,
dition xxxiii; McNeill, Churches, p. 259, considers the num-

ber "conservative"), must have far exceeded what we have
Herein Columban gives some of the freest rein to his emotion
al nature: reproaching those who flee physical, but not moral
filth; reminding his listeners of the ephemeral quality o
this life; underscoring the reward of eternity for those wh
have become dead to this world. His exhortations convey th
charged nervous overflow of the inspired teacher who makes wa
on ignorance, and by sheer might of will draws his pupils in
to the light.

Columban revetted his institutions with the facing of hi
Rules: both the so-called monastic (Regula monachorum) an
the communal (Regula coenobialis). The former is a serie
of short outlines of principle and practice categorized ac
cording to subject: on obedience, on silence, on food an
drink. Allowance is made for the strictest apportionment o
time both for each day and throughout the year: six periods
beginning in early morning and ending at midnight, at inter
vals of three hours, are set aside for prayer; the number o
psalms sung varies according to whether or not the day is th
Sabbath or Sunday, and according to the season. (See: Walker
edition, 129-31, for an outline of Columban's offices.)

The communal Rule provides an intimate look at the imple
mentation of Irish monastic discipline which was both hars
and pride-crushing. Daily confession is prescribed; the las
is liberally applied (for speaking louder than usual at table
six are in order); one's demeanor and cleanliness are judged
penance waits at every turn. Something must, however, be sai
for so strict a code. First, its popularity is beyond dis
pute--Columban was a figure commanding awe and respect; hi
disciples were many. So many that one cannot explain awa
their numbers by suggesting some sort of mass masochism. W
must remember that it was a time of undisguised brutality,whe
often little else but force was understood. The ways of de
privation are often the best weapons against discomfort an
pain; they were perhaps also the only message to be unequi
vocally clear. All in all, the challenge offered by Iris
monasticism did appeal to the heroic-minded of that age an
doubtless made civilizing progress where all else failed.

Implicit in the communal Rule, and carried to its conclu
sion in Columban's Penitential, is the principle of "contra
ries." Deriving ultimately from the so-called Methodist Schoo
of Laodicea of the 1st century B.C., but passed on to Iris
monastics by the medium of John Cassian's well-known Collo

77

ies, its basic tenet was the cure of ill by the judicious
plication of its opposite. (See: McNeill, Churches, 83-4
d 165-6.) Hence those of violent nature must learn mild-
ss; the prideful humility; the gluttonous moderation; the
stful modesty. Therein Columban also continues the tradi-
on of Finnian of Clonard whose own Penitential we apparent-
have (see: Bieler's edition, pp. 74-95), and who is men-
oned by Columban in his epistle to Gregory the Great. In
ct, it has been suggested that Columban's disciplinary work
st reflect that of his master, Comgall of Bangor (whose Rule
es not survive, but would seem to be referred to as the Ben-
uir bona regula--"Bangor's good Rule"--in the Antiphonary
Bangor; see: Gougaud, "Inventaire," 182-3).
In imposing penance for the "cure" not only of sin, but of
il inclination, Columban, like his predecessors, shows him-
lf years--centuries--ahead of his time. Apart from meting
t such punishment as strokes of the whip, periods of exile
d prayer,the Penitential (as reflected in article 12;Walker,
ition, p. 171) provides that gluttony be met with fasting,
lkativeness with silence, restlessness with "the practice
gentleness," so as to "let each suffer exactly in accord-
ce with his deserts. . . ." Regardless of what we might see
brutal, the emphasis is on reclamation, not punishment for
s own sake. McNeill has pointed out (Churches, p. 84) the
traordinary capacity, in the penitentials as a type, for
ining "social and legal heritage with scriptural morality
d severe ascetic practices." In other words, efforts such
Columban's reveal the genius of a guiding practicality, for
e sake of tempering and civilizing, within a framework of
cognizable tradition and for achievable ends.
Poetry, scholarship and law would ultimately attest the
essing of Columban's hand and of those like him. For he
s but the first whose writings we have. (See: McNeill,
nitentials, 144-5, for the Irish predecessors of Columban
the Continent.) Irish missionaries would be assumed men
learning for the very fact that they were Irish. Their
lues and vision would influence the Frankish Church (Peni-
ntials, chaps. V & VI), through it the Carolingian Empire,
d through it Europe. A 14th-century singer of Christian
pire and poet of cosmic vision, Dante, would see the undo-
g of evil by the exercise of its opposite as the secret to
rgatory.
More immediately, Gall founded the great monastery which

bears his name. In 680 the Lombards embraced Rome.   Bobbi
gift of the Arian King Agilulf, by then had been enjoying
unique papal privilege for over fifty years, and was earni
its reputation for scholarship. The intractable, impertinen
irascible,energetic and somehow engaging Columban--pilgrim f
Christ--had found his place of resurrection.

*   *   *

BIBLIOGRAPHY
(with abbreviations)

A.O. and M.O. Anderson, Adomnan's Life of Columba, London a
    New York: Thomas Nelson and Sons Ltd, 1961.
Annals of Inisfallen, ed. Sean Mac Airt, Dublin, 1951.(AI)
Annals of Tigernach, ed. Whitley Stokes,<Revue Celtique> X
    (1895), 374-419; XVII (1896),6-33,116-263, 337-420;XVI
    (1897), 9-59, 150-303, 374-91. (AT)
Annals of Ulster, ed. W.M. Hennessy, Dublin, 1897-1901. (A
Bede, Opera Historica, trans.by J.E. King,2 vols.,Wm.Heinema
    Ltd and Harvard University Press: London and Cambridge,rp
    1971 & 1963. (Ecclesiastical History: EH)
Ludwig Bieler, The Life and Legend of St. Patrick,Dublin,194
    "   "   , "The Humanism of St.Columbanus," <Mélanges
                Columbiens>, Paris, 1951, pp. 95-102. (Humanism
    "   "   , The Works of Saint Patrick, Ancient Christi
                Writers, Newman Press: Westminster,Maryland,196
    "   "   ed., The Irish Penitentials, Scriptores Latin
    Hiberniae,The Dublin Institute for Advanced Studies:Dubli
    1975. (Penitentials or Bieler)
Daniel A. Binchy, "Patrick and his Biographers: Ancient a
    Modern," <Studia Hibernica> 2, 1962, pp. 1-173.
J.B. Bury, Life of Saint Patrick, London, 1905.
James Carney, The Problem of Saint Patrick, The Dublin Inst
    tute for Advanced Studies: Dublin, 1961. (Carney)
Nora K. Chadwick, Poetry and Letters in Early Christian Gau
                Bowes and Bowes: London, 1955. (P&L)

ra K. Chadwick, The Age of the Saints in the Early Celtic
Church, Oxford University Press: London 1961. (Saints or
Chadwick)
en Chadwick, John Cassian, Cambridge University Press, 2nd
edition, 1968. (Cassian)
ronicon Scotorum, Rolls S., ed. W. M.Hennessy, London, 1866.
(CS)
rgaret Deanesly, A History of Early Medieval Europe from 476
to 911, London and New York: Methuen & Co. Ltd and Barnes &
Noble Inc., rpt. 1963. (HEME)
and L. De Paor, Early Christian Ireland, London, 1958.
les Dillon ed., Early Irish Society, Dublin: At the Sign of
the Three Candles, 1954.
les Dillon and Nora K. Chadwick, The Celtic Realms, The New
American Library: New York, 1967. (D&C)
D. Douglas ed., The New International Dictionary of the
Christian Church,The Paternoster Press: Exeter,1975.(NIDCC)
th Dudley Edwards, An Atlas of Irish History,Methuen: London
and New York, 2nd edition, 1981. (Dudley Edwards)
edegarius, The Fourth Book of the Chronicle of Fredegar,
trans. J.M. Wallace-Hadrill, Thomas Nelson and Sons Ltd:
London and New York, 1960.
uis Gougaud,"Inventaire des règles monastiques irlandaises,"
<Revue Bénédictine>, 1908, no.2, pp. 167-84; no.3,
321-33.("Inventaire")
Greene, "Some Linguistic Evidence relating to the British
Church," <Christianity in Britain 300-700>, ed. M. Barley
and R.P.C. Hanson, Leicester, 1968, pp. 75-86.
egory Bishop of Tours, History of the Franks, trans. Ernest
Brehaut, W.W.Norton & Co. Inc., New York, 1969.
W. Haddan and W. Stubbs, Councils and Ecclesiastical Docu-
ments relating to Great Britain and Ireland, 3 vols., Ox-
ford,1869-73.
P.C. Hanson, Saint Patrick: His Origins and Career, Claren-
          don Press: Oxford, 1968.
  "   "   , Saint Patrick,Confession et Lettre à Coroticus,
Les Editions du Cerf: Paris, 1978. (Confession, Letter, or
Hanson)
W. Heist, Vitae Sanctorum Hiberniae, Subsidia hagiographica,
28, Brussels, 1965. (Heist)
thleen Hughes, The Church in Early Irish Society, Cornell
          University Press: Ithaca, New York,1966. (CEIS)
  "   "   , Early Christian Ireland, Cornell University

Press: Ithaca, New York, 1972. (ECI)

Kathleen Hughes and Ann Hamlin, The Modern Traveller to t
Early Irish Church, SPCK: London, 1977. (Hughes and Hamli

Kenneth H.Jackson,Language and History in Early Britain, Edi
burgh University Press: Edinburgh, 1953. (LHEB)

Jonas, Vita Columbani, ed. B. Krusch, M.G.H., Scriptores Rer
Merovingicarum, iv, 1902.

James F. Kenney,The Sources for the Early History of Irelan
Ecclesiastical, ed. Ludwig Bieler, rpt. Octagon Press: N
York, 1966. (Sources)

Thomas Kinsella, trans., The Tain, Oxford University Pres
London and New York, 1970.

Hans Lietzmann, A History of the Early Church: IV: The Era
the Church Fathers, trans. Bertram Lee Woolf, World Pub-
lishing Company, Meridian Books: Cleveland and New York,
1953. (Lietzmann)

Eoin MacNeill, Saint Patrick,Apostle of Ireland, ed.John Rya
Clonmore and Reynolds: Dublin, 1964.

Gearoid Mac Niocaill, Ireland before the Vikings, Gill and M
Millan Ltd: Dublin and London, 1972.

John T. McNeill, The Celtic Penitentials, Edouard Champio
Paris, 1923.

    "   "   , The Celtic Churches: A History, A.D. 200
1200, University of Chicago Press: Chicago and London,197
(Churches)

Christine Mohrmann, The Latin of Saint Patrick, The Dublin I
stitute for Advanced Studies: Dublin, 1961. (LSP)

John Morris, "The Dates of the Celtic Saints," <Journal
Theological Studies> N.S., vol. 17, pt. 2, Octob
1966, 342-91.

    "   "   , The Age of Arthur, Charles Scribner's Sons: N
York, 1973.

Thomas F. O'Rahilly, The Two Patricks: A Lecture on the Hi
tory of Christianity in Fifth-Century Ir
land, The Dublin Institute for Advanced
Studies: Dublin, 1942.

    "   "   , Early Irish History and Mythology, T
Dublin Institute for Advanced Studies: Dublin, 1946. (EIH

T. O'Raifeartaigh, "Saint Patrick's Twenty-eight Days' Jou
ney," <Irish Historical Studies> 64 (1969), 395-416.

P. O'Riain, "Boundary Association in Early Irish Society,"
<Studia Celtica> VII (1972), 12-29.

Charles Plummer ed., Vitae Sanctorum Hiberniae, 2 vols.,Oxfo

University Press: Oxford, rpt. 1968. (VSH)

dward K. Rand,Founders of the Middle Ages,Dover Publications:
    New York, new edition 1957.

. Ryan, Irish Monasticism, its Origins and Early Development,
    London, 1931.

.W. Smit, Studies in the Language and Style of Columba the
    Younger, Amsterdam, 1971.

aitley Stokes ed.,"The Bodleian <Amra Choluimb Chille>," <Re-
    vue Celtique> XX (1899), 30-55, 132-83, 248-89, 400-37; XXI
    (1900) 133-6.

aarles Thomas, Britain and Ireland in Early Christian Times:
    A.D. 400-800, McGraw-Hill: New York, 1971. (ECT)

.S.M. Walker, "On the Use of Greek Words in the Writings of
            St. Columbanus of Luxeuil," <Bulletin du Cange>
            XXI (1951), 117-31. (Use)

    "   "   ed., Sancti Columbani Opera, The Dublin Insti-
    tute for Advanced Studies: Dublin, rpt. 1970. (ed. Walker)

MAP II:

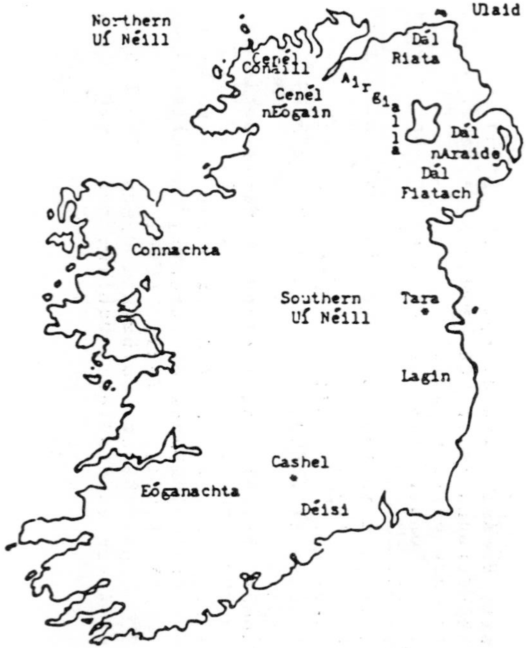

Northern Uí Néill

Cenél Conaill
Cenél nEógain
Airgialla
Dál Riata
Dál nAraide
Dál Fiatach
Ulaid

Connachta

Tara
Southern Uí Néill
Lagin

Cashel
Eóganachta
Déisi

MAP I:

Iona
Argyll
Galloway
Hadrian's Wall
Carlisle
Whithorn
Man
Ulaid

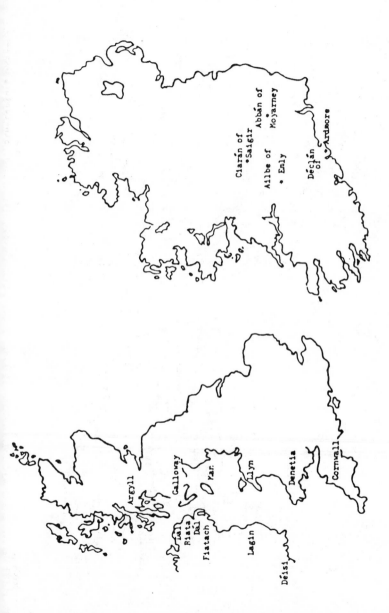

MAP III:

5th-Century Irish Migrations

MAP IV:

Early Missionaries in the South of Ireland

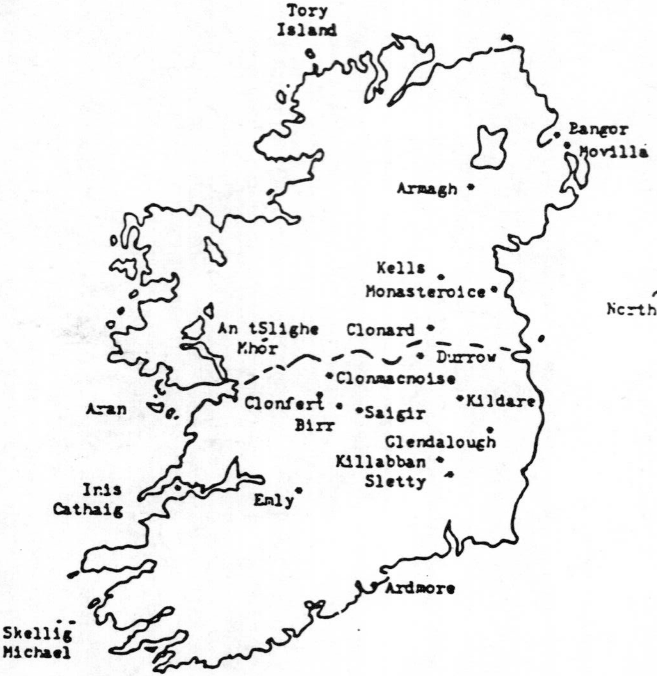

Tory
Island

Bangor•
•Movilla

Armagh•

Kells
Monasterboice•

Clonard• Durrow•

•Kildare

An tSlighe
Mhór

•Clonmacnoise

Clonfert• •Saigir
Birr

Glendalough

Killabban•
Sletty•

Aran

Enly•
Iris
Cathaig

•Ardmore

Skellig
Michael

Inverness•

Picts

Tul
Plata
Iona•

Britons Anglo-
Saxons

Mar.

North. Neill'd

MAP VI:

MAP VII: